The Media Industry

Proceedings of the AIMR seminar *The Media Industry*

January 31–February 1, 1996
New York, New York

Peter P. Appert, CFA
Christoper P. Dixon
James D. Dougherty, CFA
Mario J. Gabelli, CFA
Lawrence J. Haverty, Jr., CFA
Dennis H. Leibowitz

Andrew W. Marcus, CFA, *Moderator*
Sumner M. Redstone
George Reed-Dellinger
John S. Reidy, CFA
Mayo T. Smith
Susan V. Watson, CFA

> To obtain the *AIMR Publications Catalog*, contact:
> AIMR, P.O. Box 3668, Charlottesville, Virginia 22903, U.S.A.
> Phone 804-980-3668; Fax 804-980-9775; E-mail info@aimr.com
> or
> visit AIMR's World Wide Web site at **http: //www.aimr.com/aimr.html**
> to view the AIMR publications list.

©1996, Association for Investment Management and Research

All rights reserved. No part of this publication may be reproduced, stored in a retrieval system, or transmitted, in any form or by any means, electronic, mechanical, photocopying, recording, or otherwise, without prior written permission of the copyright holder.

ICFA Continuing Education is published monthly eight times a year in January, April, May, June, August, September, October, and November by the Association for Investment Management and Research, P.O. Box 3668, Charlottesville, Virginia 22903, U.S.A. This publication is designed to provide accurate and authoritative information with regard to the subject matter covered. It is sold with the understanding that the publisher is not engaged in rendering legal, accounting, or other professional services. If legal advice or other expert assistance is required, the services of a competent professional should be sought. Periodical postage paid at the post office in Richmond, Virginia, and additional mailing offices.

Copies are mailed as a benefit of membership to CFA® charterholders. Subscriptions also are available at US$100 for one year. Address all circulation communications to ICFA Continuing Education, P.O. Box 3668, Charlottesville, Virginia 22903, U.S.A.; Phone 804-980-3668; Fax 804-980-9775. For change of address, send mailing label and new address six weeks in advance.

Postmaster: Send address changes to the Association for Investment Management and Research, P.O. Box 3668, Charlottesville, Virginia 22903.

ISBN 1-879087-69-3
Printed in the United States of America
June 1996

Editorial Staff
Sanjiv Bhatia
Vice President, Educational Products

Charlene Semer
Editor

Jaynee M. Dudley
Manager, Educational Products

Roger Mitchell
Assistant Editor

Lois Carrier
Typesetting/Layout

Contents

Foreword	v
Katrina F. Sherrerd, CFA	
Biographies of Speakers	vi
The Media Industry: An Overview	1
Sanjiv Bhatia	
Company-Specific Strategic Issues	5
Sumner M. Redstone	
The Regulatory Environment	12
George Reed-Dellinger	
The Media in 2005	19
Dennis H. Leibowitz	
Distinguishing Characteristics of the Publishing Sector	28
Peter P. Appert, CFA	
The Advertising Sector	47
James D. Dougherty, CFA	
Changes in the Industry Dynamics	59
Christopher P. Dixon	
Broadcast and Cable Television Sectors	72
Andrew W. Marcus, CFA	
A Valuation Framework	82
Mario J. Gabelli, CFA	
Mayo T. Smith	
Interpreting the Industry Numbers	87
Lawrence J. Haverty, Jr., CFA	
The Art of the Interview	95
John S. Reidy, CFA	
Susan V. Watson, CFA	

ICFA Board of Trustees, 1995–96

Abby Joseph Cohen, CFA, *Chair*
New York, New York

Frank K. Reilly, CFA, *Vice Chair*
Notre Dame, Indiana

Thomas L. Hansberger, CFA, *AIMR Chair*
Ft. Lauderdale, Florida

I. Rossa O'Reilly, CFA, *AIMR Vice Chair*
Toronto, Ontario, Canada

Thomas A. Bowman, CFA, *AIMR President and CEO*
Charlottesville, Virginia

John A. Gunn, CFA
San Francisco, California

John L. Maginn, CFA
Omaha, Nebraska

Thomas P. Moore, Jr., CFA
Boston, Massachusetts

George W. Noyes, CFA*
Boston, Massachusetts

Fred H. Speece, Jr., CFA
Minneapolis, Minnesota

Joan P. Trapnell, CFA
Boston, Massachusetts

Eliot P. Williams, CFA
Hartford, Connecticut

Brian F. Wruble, CFA
New York, New York

ex officio

AIMR Education Committee, 1995–96

Eliot P. Williams, CFA, *Chair*
Hartford, Connecticut

Fred H. Speece, Jr., CFA, *Vice Chair*
Minneapolis, Minnesota

Frank K. Reilly, CFA, *Vice Chair*
Notre Dame, Indiana

Thomas A. Bowman, CFA
Charlottesville, Virginia

Keith C. Brown, CFA
Austin, Texas

Dwight D. Churchill, CFA
Boston, Massachusetts

Abby Joseph Cohen, CFA
New York, New York

Charles F. O'Connell, CFA
Chicago, Illinois

Terence V. Pavlic, CFA
Columbus, Ohio

I. Rossa O'Reilly, CFA
Toronto, Ontario, Canada

Katrina F. Sherrerd, CFA
Charlottesville, Virginia

J. Clay Singleton, CFA
Charlottesville, Virginia

AIMR Senior Education Staff

Thomas A. Bowman, CFA
President and CEO

Katrina F. Sherrerd, CFA
Senior Vice President

J. Clay Singleton, CFA
Senior Vice President

Sanjiv Bhatia
Vice President

Julia S. Hammond, CFA
Vice President

Robert M. Luck, Jr., CFA
Vice President

Aaron L. Shackelford, CFA
Vice President

Donald L. Tuttle, CFA
Vice President

Barbara L. Higgins
Director

Paul W. Turner
Director

Foreword

The old saying "timing is everything" is an appropriate theme for this proceedings of *The Media Industry* seminar, which ended on February 1, 1996, the day the Telecommunications Act of 1996 was passed in the U.S. Senate. As the ninth seminar in the Industry Analysis series, *The Media Industry* was true to the series' guiding principle of introducing the basic structure and environment of a particular industry—in this case, the broadcasting, cable television, publishing, and advertising sectors of the media industry.

The timing of this seminar was excellent for reasons other than simply coinciding with passage of the Telecommunications Act. In recent years, this industry has been changing dramatically through its involvement in the revolution in information delivery, but the future of the industry depends on more than technology alone. Today, technological advances are combining with the emergence of new markets to globalize the industry and create new media outlets. Radical structural change is under way as companies consolidate to acquire the increased size and scale necessary to compete globally. As a result of such trends, the traditional lines between companies and industry sectors are blurring. The situation is complicated by the Telecommunications Act, which introduces regulatory changes that will benefit some industry sectors but may hinder others.

The speakers in this proceedings address the fundamental structure and environment of the media industry, present their opinions on the future, offer insights into valuation strategies appropriate to the special circumstances of this industry, and provide guidance on the art of interviewing companies in the media industry. We wish to thank Andrew W. Marcus, CFA, of Alex. Brown & Sons for serving both as the moderator of the seminar and as a presenter. For their valuable contributions, we also extend our thanks to Peter P. Appert, CFA, Alex. Brown & Sons; Christopher P. Dixon, PaineWebber; James D. Dougherty, CFA, Dean Witter Reynolds; Mario J. Gabelli, CFA, Gabelli Funds; Lawrence J. Haverty, Jr., CFA, State Street Research and Management Company; Dennis H. Leibowitz, Donaldson, Lufkin & Jenrette; Sumner M. Redstone, Viacom; George Reed-Dellinger, HSBC Washington Analysis; John S. Reidy, CFA, Smith Barney, Inc.; Mayo T. Smith, Gabelli & Company; and Susan V. Watson, CFA, Gannett Company.

Previous AIMR Industry Analysis seminars covered the automotive, consumer staples, financial services, heath care, oil and gas, retail, telecommunications, and transportation industries. Core topics in each series seminar include analysis of the internal and external factors that affect each sector, interpretation of the numbers, and valuation of the securities. Proceedings from these seminars are also available and may be previewed in the catalog section of AIMR's World Wide Web site (**http://www.aimr.com/aimr.html**). We invite you to review the entire series if you have not done so already.

Katrina F. Sherrerd, CFA
Senior Vice President
Educational Products

Biographies of Speakers

Peter P. Appert, CFA, is managing director of the research division at Alex. Brown & Sons. He holds a B.A. in economics from Lafayette College, an M.A. in economics from New York University, and an M.B.A. from Stanford University.

Christopher P. Dixon is a managing director of Paine Webber and currently serves as group coordinator for the Communications Equity Research Group. He is a graduate of the University of Pennsylvania and holds an M.B.A. in finance from the Stern School of Business at New York University.

James D. Dougherty, CFA, is a senior vice president at Dean Witter Reynolds. Prior to joining Dean Witter Reynolds, he served as an analyst for NatWest Markets. Mr. Dougherty holds an A.B. in history from Colgate University and an M.B.A. in marketing from the Wharton School of the University of Pennsylvania.

Mario J. Gabelli, CFA, is chairman of Gabelli Funds. He is a graduate of Fordham University and holds an M.B.A. from the Columbia University Graduate School of Business and an honorary doctorate degree from Roger Williams University.

Lawrence J. Haverty, Jr., CFA, is senior vice president at State Street Research and Management Company and a member of the firm's Equity Research Group. Prior to joining State Street, he held positions at Putnam Investments and Fred Alger Management. Mr. Haverty holds a B.S. and an M.A. from the University of Pennsylvania.

Dennis H. Leibowitz is a senior vice president and securities analyst at Donaldson, Lufkin & Jenrette. He holds a B.S. in economics from the University of Pennsylvania and is a graduate of the Wharton School of the University of Pennsylvania.

Andrew W. Marcus, CFA, is a managing director of Alex. Brown & Sons and a member of the Media/Communications Research Group. He holds an A.B in economics from the University of Michigan.

Sumner M. Redstone is chairman of the board, president, and chief executive officer of National Amusements, the parent company of Viacom, and also serves as chairman of the board of Viacom. After two and a half years at Harvard College, he received a degree from Harvard University's Special Board of Overseers and holds an L.L.B. from the Harvard University School of Law.

George Reed-Dellinger is vice president and telemedia analyst at HSBC Washington Analysis. Previously, he served as adjunct professor of international business at American University. Mr. Dellinger holds B.S. and M.B.A. degrees from American University.

John S. Reidy, CFA, is a managing director and senior analyst at Smith Barney Inc. He holds an A.B. in political science from Harvard College and an M.B.A. from Harvard Business School.

Mayo T. Smith is assistant vice president and manager of institutional sales at Gabelli & Company. Prior to joining Gabelli & Company in 1993, he served as southeast region sales representative for the Moen Inc. division of American Brands and was also employed by R.J. Reynolds. Mr. Smith holds an undergraduate degree from Muhlenberg College.

Susan V. Watson, CFA, is vice president of investor relations at the Gannett Company. Prior to joining Gannett, she served as a media analyst at Morgan Stanley & Company. Ms. Watson has also served on the board of supervisors of the National Investor Relations Institute. She is a graduate of the University of Southern California.

The Media Industry: An Overview

Sanjiv Bhatia
Vice President, Educational Products

If the predictions of some observers are correct, as Andrew Marcus notes in his presentation, the media industry will be the second largest U.S. industry, behind aerospace, by the end of this century. Consolidation, vertical integration, new delivery platforms, bundled distribution, branded networks, leveraged content, gatekeeping—these are but a sample of the phenomena affecting the media industry. The prosperity of individual companies or even whole sectors may depend, however, on such unpredictable variables as national and international regulatory environments. Although impressive technical jargon permeates discussions of this industry, the hype, as Sumner Redstone emphasizes in his presentation, is often very different from the reality. The presentations in this proceedings address the cutting-edge issues in a user-friendly manner. The speakers find that successful analysis consists of adapting tried-and-true techniques to gain insights into such familiar areas as franchise value, operating expenses, and cash flow.

The Telecommunications Act of 1996

The publication of this proceedings presented the awkward fact that the conference was held a week prior to the enactment of the Telecommunications Act of 1996. So, although every attempt has been made to make the presentations appear *ex post*, please bear in mind that the participants' comments, from which this proceedings have been written, were made prior to the bill becoming law.

This overview of the sections of the act pertinent to the media industry is intended to obviate any confusion about the legislation. The act accomplishes the following:
- Removes legal barriers separating nearly a dozen telemedia sectors.
- Drops the provision that would have eliminated the numerous cross-ownership rules that restrict mergers between most subsectors of the media industry.
- Gives the go-ahead to deals in the area of radio broadcasting that had been put on hold.
- Repeals the statutory ban against TV networks owning cable systems.
- Eliminates the ownership ceiling of 12 TV stations, and increases from 25 percent to 35 percent the permissible coverage of the nation's households.
- Prohibits "in-region" combinations between overlapping telco/cable operators, except in rural areas with populations less than 50,000.
- Allows the Bell Operating Companies (BOCs) to undergo pro-competitive restructuring but conditions their entry into long distance. The act forces BOCs to let long-distance companies into the local arena before the BOCs themselves can offer long-distance services.
- Removes long-distance bans against the provision of incidental services (cellular) and out-of-region services (resale) by long-distance companies.
- Increases the existing incentives to "bypass" access service charges paid to local telephone companies.
- Preserves the Federal Communications Commission 25 percent ceiling on "alien" ownership of U.S. companies controlling licenses for the use of spectrum.
- Postpones action on saddling TV broadcasters with incremental spectrum costs.

The Media Industry

Sumner Redstone believes four important factors will shape the future of this industry. The first key development is the Telecommunications Act, the immediate effect of which will be a spate of consolidations as restrictions on radio and television station ownership are relaxed. Second, the globalization of the media industry will provide new outlets for domestic products and services, often at a very cheap entry price. The third major force is the sweep and impact of new technologies, such as the growth of the Internet. The fourth force involves the issue of size, scale, and power as media becomes an increasingly global industry. Redstone concludes that an effective leadership structure is critical to company success in the media industry—now more than ever before.

In his presentation, George Reed-Dellinger reviews the Telecommunications Act and tries to determine who the big winners and losers might be from this legislation. He predicts that the act is likely to trigger a wave of takeover activity among major companies and will affect roughly 20 percent of the S&P 500 Index companies.

According to Reed-Dellinger, the new legislation appears tilted in favor of the television broadcasters, and investors will probably find attractive opportunities in smaller, independent TV stations that could be taken over as a result of the elimination of the network 12-station rule. In addition, the elimination of the financial interest and syndication rules, or Fin-Syn, will benefit TV broadcasters, making them the likely big winners of the new legislation. Reed-Dellinger sees cable companies gaining least from regulatory changes and expects them to be "flipped out of the regulatory frying pan into the competitive skillet." The new act will also open up the local telephone markets to competition. AT&T and MCI are likely to benefit from the new regulatory environment, but Reed-Dellinger doubts the Bell companies will enjoy success as great as some observers have forecast.

Dennis Leibowitz looks into his crystal ball and presents the industry outlook for the year 2005. He believes that regulation, technological change, internationalization, and structural change are important factors behind what is occurring in the media and communications business. Specifically, Leibowitz predicts that joint ventures designed to combine cable and telephone services will be a prominent feature of the future media industry.

Leibowitz believes the big winners in the wake of the Telecommunications Act are likely to be the content providers such as software producers and entertainment companies. Telephone companies stand to gain the least, because market share shifts are likely to come at their expense. The cable sector may be a middle case, but Leibowitz believes new opportunities could outweigh possible losses in this sector.

The Newspaper and Book-Publishing Sector

Peter Appert's presentation deals with the publishing sector, particularly the newspaper and book-publishing subsectors. During the past few years, the growth rate in publishing has lagged the growth of GDP, but any suggestion of the death of the print media is premature. Appert highlights four main factors affecting the publishing industry: cyclical pressures, technology, competition, and consolidation.

In newspapers, the developments to watch are technology and consolidation. Advances in technology have allowed newspapers to control labor costs while increasing productivity, and opportunities in electronic distribution will allow some publishers to leverage their content—that is, to sell the same news more than once. Appert points out that most newspapers now have virtual monopolies in their markets as a result of consolidations and business failures. This development has been a boon to cash flow margins of survivors.

The segment to focus on in book publishing is educational/professional publishing, which has high operating margins (mid- to high teens), high barriers to entry, and predictable revenue dynamics. The key drivers among educational publishers are demographics and textbook adoption decisions by states—both fairly predictable events. Like newspapers, professional publishers face the happy prospect of leveraging their products through new distribution channels.

Future valuations must also take into account the continuing industry consolidation. About 10–15 years ago, the educational publishing industry consisted of a dozen or so major players; now, only four to six major players remain. Significant economies of scale have encouraged market share growth via acquisition.

The Advertising Sector

James Dougherty's presentation indicates that the advertising group has generally underperformed the S&P 500 during the past 10 years but that successful companies can provide good performance. Dougherty focuses his analysis on operating expenses. Companies that control salaries and related expenses and maintain operating profits at a certain ratio to interest will enjoy solid growth in earnings per share.

Dougherty notes that much of the growth in advertising will come from Latin America and Asia, but changes in the nature of the business will lead to new opportunities in the United States. From a standard model in which clients have only such basic needs as promotion and brand identity, the business is evolving toward a new model in which advertisers deal in clients' logistical concerns. Advertisers are also using technology such as digital distribution and interactive networks to create new niches. Dougherty believes that the only factor preventing the World Wide Web from becoming a significant source of advertising revenue is the lack of a credible third-party measuring system, which is well on the way to becoming a reality.

The Broadcast and Cable Television Sectors

Christopher Dixon's presentation focuses on changes in industry dynamics. Specifically, he details two potential models for the communications business of the next century. In the "library model," content is king. A company owns a proprietary data base, archive, or program library, which it licenses to a variety of users for fees that differ according to the medium used to deliver the product. The second model—which Dixon dubs "gatekeeping"—emphasizes distribution. The intent is to develop subscriber bases and collect fees based on customized offerings. The bundling of video, data, and voice services in the gatekeeping model is an attempt to hold on to current customers in the face of emerging competition and at the same time develop new business lines.

In his presentation, Andrew Marcus discusses industry themes and growth trends in the broadcast and cable television sectors. He points out that television stocks have outperformed the market for the past three years and that the basic reason for this outperformance is regulatory relief. Marcus expects the Telecommunications Act to bring rapid consolidation within the sector, allowing television groups to purchase programming less expensively, share overhead, and use size as a comparative advantage in dealing with capital markets.

In recent years, the radio sector has had rapidly rising private market values and has experienced some of the fastest growth in free cash flow among media sectors. Radio's recent gains in advertising share may pale in comparison to the benefits Marcus expects to accrue to this sector as a result of the Telecommunications Act. Changes in ownership restrictions will allow clustering—ownership of multiple stations in the same market. The result will be greater profitability because a company can use clusters to dominate whole formats. The risk is also lower because of less competition, and size can also result in shared overhead and greater access to financing.

Some key factors to consider when valuing radio broadcasting stocks are diversification, internal growth, station cash flow growth, and companies' acquisition histories. Marcus warns against companies that get too highly leveraged, his litmus test being a ratio of debt to earnings before interest, taxes, depreciation, and amortization (EBITDA) of about 6 times.

Marcus characterizes recent growth in the wired cable sector as "solid but slow." During the past few years, the cable sector has experienced new competition in the form of wireless cable, telephone companies, private cable, and DBS (direct broadcast satellite) services. The Telecommunications Act will ease FCC supervision somewhat and allow cable companies to venture into telephony. As a result, the sector's capital expenditures likely will continue to be high. Companies will need to be large and have abundant resources if they are to remain competitive, so consolidation in this sector is likely to continue.

Although the wireless cable sector is small, Marcus considers it a niche business with great potential. He ranks quality of management as especially important in this sector. Companies must manage their balance sheets prudently and face the difficult challenge of controlling marketing costs in a developing business that is still trying to increase its subscriber base. Wireless cable has specific competitive advantages in its ability to serve customers better than wired cable and its viability in areas where cable competition is weak or nonexistent.

A Guide to Valuing Media Stocks

The rapidly changing structure of the media industry and the companies within it makes stock valuation particularly difficult. Rapidly developing global opportunities, major players outside the United States, and the instant and free flow of information worldwide all add to the complexity of the valuation process. How does this configuration translate into profits for clients? Lawrence Haverty, Mario Gabelli, and Mayo Smith discuss various valuation techniques that work well with media stocks.

The Classical Approach

In their presentation, Mario Gabelli and Mayo Smith point out that as companies see rising economic activity and profits, gaps are likely to develop between the public market price of a stock and the private market value of the business. New takeover activity and mergers will refocus attention on the franchise values of companies in this industry.

Gabelli and Smith suggest a fundamentalist approach, investing primarily in the equities of cash-generating franchise companies that are selling in the public market at significant discounts to the fundamental appraisals of their intrinsic values. Their approach to fundamental research is three pronged: free cash flow (EBITDA) minus the capital expenditures necessary to grow the business; earnings per share trends; and private market value, which encompasses on- and off-balance-sheet assets and liabilities. Adjustments are made to these valuations to account for management changes that may energize lazy assets, which is especially critical in a rapidly changing industry such as media in which valuations are subject to rapid change as ownerships change hands. As with any industry, identifying the catalysts that will cause changes in valuation is important: for the media industry, the catalysts may be the regulatory environment and merger and acquisition activity.

Enterprise Value Analysis

Lawrence Haverty argues that media companies are too complex for traditional analysis and that conventional accounting does not work for entertainment companies. He prescribes an analytical framework better suited to understanding the industry from an investment standpoint—a methodology called enterprise value analysis (EVA). Enterprise value is defined as the market value of equity, less cash and hidden assets, and plus debt. The value multiple is created by dividing the enterprise value by the four-quarter trailing EBITDA.

Although this approach has its pitfalls, it is a simple technique that requires calculating only a few variables:
- A trailing EBITD plus debt and less cash.
- An estimate of hidden assets and an estimate of company growth.

Armed with this information, analysts can calculate the EVA for each company and then rank companies by three variables: the ratio of total growth to the enterprise value multiple, EBITD growth, and total growth. The companies at the top are generally the ones to buy, and the companies at the bottom are the ones to sell.

The Art of the Interview

The final part of this proceedings is an interesting interplay between John Reidy, who plays the role of a media analyst, and Susan Watson, who plays the role of an investor relations (IR) officer. The two address some of the major faux pas that analysts make when visiting a firm to collect information. They discuss basic rules, from preparation to developing a good relationship with the IR officer and staff, and suggest strategies that might make this seemingly painful task more pleasant both for analysts and for IR officers.

Conclusion

In general, these presentations share a clear consensus about the major developments shaping this industry: globalization, consolidation, regulation, technology. Despite such momentous factors, the crucial difference between excellence and mediocrity may be something almost humble in comparison. To the list of driving forces, Sumner Redstone adds another and—in his opinion—decisive factor: management. All the speakers discuss management's function in the various sectors and some even highlight the need for "entrepreneurial" leadership, but only Redstone asserts the preeminence of management. "Business success will always be determined by visionaries," he notes, "people who can cull existing facts and historical knowledge to form an appreciation for what is likely to happen in the future and then act on it."

Certainly, the managements of media companies will not suffer from a lack of growth potential if this industry is to become the second largest U.S. industry by the year 2000. In a period of such leavening, the question is, of course, who the winners and losers will be. The challenge for media companies, in Christopher Dixon's words, "will be how to structure the firm internally to ration capital and maximize shareholder returns while taking advantage of a cornucopia of opportunity." The presentations in this proceedings offer some of the tools necessary for scoring companies' progress toward that end.

Company-Specific Strategic Issues

Sumner M. Redstone
Chairman and Chief Executive Officer
Viacom, Inc.

> Four key developments are likely to affect the media industry in the future: the Telecommunications Act of 1996, the globalization of the industry, the impact of new distribution technologies, and the need for size and scale in the new media landscape. In this rapidly changing global environment, being bigger and more powerful is essential to mitigate risks, create leverage, and take advantage of scale. By the year 2000, a handful of global media giants likely will dominate the industry.

The much-hyped technological revolution is upon us. We live in a world where the international marketplace is exploding and where an awesome and growing concentration of power presents enormous opportunities and corresponding hazards and challenges. The operations of Viacom are now more diverse and complicated, with evolving ventures all over the world, not to mention a challenging studio business on the West Coast. Success in that world requires more than ever a nimble, aggressive, entrepreneurial, highly focused, and opportunistic leadership structure, and that is exactly what we have today at Viacom. The team that surrounds me combines creative, diverse, and in-depth management expertise; talent relations; marketing savvy; and track record in building world-class brands to distinguish Viacom as the preeminent content provider in the world.

The State of Technology

We are now exactly midway between the advent of the 1990s and the most ballyhooed date in modern times—the year 2000. We can both look back five years to the beginning of the 1990s and look forward another five to the next millennium.

So much has happened in the media and telecommunications industry in the last five years, and then again, so much has not. As we compare the events of the decade with the pronouncements that ushered it in, we see any number of interesting twists of fate: predictions that failed to develop, developments that defied the predictions.

The future, it seems, is an elusive beast. Just as we feel its breath upon our necks, we turn to discover it is still some distance away. And that has certainly been our experience in the 1990s.

Not so long ago, we were told that technology would imminently transform the way we live, work, and entertain ourselves. Soon we would be surfing 500 channels of television fare while shopping via PC and receiving our medical care through video teleconferencing.

The suburban mall was doomed, as was the book. Indeed, the notion of a centralized government seemed almost an anachronism in light of the emerging Internet electorate. Only a couple of years ago, everyone seemed to agree that interactive television would fundamentally transfigure our society overnight, that slumbering couch potatoes would suddenly seize the remote and start transacting in digital bits and bytes, that high-speed networks would revamp public services and rejuvenate the American economy.

The reality is that we are nowhere near a 500-channel universe, largely because consumers do not want it. Single lanes of interactivity and multimedia have emerged, but they are far from the information superhighway once envisioned. The computer and the television have *not* converged; we do not have universal video teleconferencing or smart homes (unless you are Bill Gates); and most people still look to the stores or catalogs, not the Internet or online services, to do their shopping. Yet I assert we are standing at a historic crossroads: Our society *is* being reshaped by powerful new technologies of light and silicon, our national and cultural boundaries are being redefined, and these changes will transform the personal futures of everyone.

Although certain predictions have not come to pass, others have already been borne out. A third of American households now have a personal computer, and tens of millions of them access the Internet. Technological advancements such as digitization, fiber optics, cellular services, and CD-ROMs—which had been prophesied—are today a reality, and the world has, in fact, become a global village.

The pace of change may be more evolutionary than revolutionary, but its scope is no less profound than originally contemplated. The next few decades will witness fundamental alterations not only in the way we live, work, and entertain ourselves but also in the strategies of businesses, the dynamics of the marketplace, the competition between companies and between countries, even the role of government. So, where does that leave us? Beyond all the industry slang—surfing the Net, vertical integration, content versus distribution—real and tangible forces are at work in our industry.

I would like to put aside the hype and the headlines and take a sober and informed look at what is ahead for our industry as we complete this decade and enter the next century. The next several years will undoubtedly prove to be the most exciting and challenging yet. The opportunities and potential rewards are huge, but they also carry with them complex challenges, not the least of which is discerning what is real and what is hype.

The Media Industry

Four key developments in our business are very *real* and very potent:
- In the short term—today—the signing into law of the telecommunications bill.
- In the intermediate term—this year—the sweeping globalization of our business.
- Over the long term—this decade—the impact of new distribution technologies, particularly the Internet.
- As a consequence of the first three developments, the need for size, scale, and sheer power in this new media landscape, and the need to know how to exercise that power effectively.

The Telecommunications Act

The first key development is in the short term—today. What is *real* today is that the most sweeping telecommunications legislation to be enacted in this country in 70 years has become law. In brief, it is procompetitive, it will open up new markets, and it will benefit consumers—that is, after they recover from the telemarketing tidal wave that will overcome them.

What is also real is the fact that the enactment of this legislation is only the beginning. Before our industry or consumers see or feel any difference in telecommunications providers, new ground rules must be established, further defining competition and setting rate structures. Only when this task has been accomplished, sometime during the next 12–18 months, will we be likely to see the new round of mergers this legislation is expected to spark.

The consolidation in cable will continue. The urge to merge will spread to telephony as regulatory barriers come hurtling down. As restrictions on radio and television station ownership are relaxed, vertical integration within local markets will increase.

All in all, telecommunications deregulation will not only open up the playing field, it will open up the pipeline into consumer households. It will encourage new, more potent distribution systems in video, voice, and data, and that development will benefit not only consumers but also any and all content providers.

As distribution systems proliferate, content—compelling, branded, got-to-have content—becomes even more important and vital. And Congress has just powerfully reaffirmed that. It is not what it is on but what is on it that counts. That is what is *real* today and tomorrow. Think about the effect on companies such as Viacom as new direct broadcast satellites rise in the sky and as more distribution systems on the land, such as the telephone companies, seek video programming as a road to success.

Globalization

The second key force affects the intermediate term—this year. What is *real* this year is the globalization of our business.

We can no longer afford to think in domestic terms, nor can we ship canned American product overseas and call that an effective global strategy. Already, foreign cash flow growth in film, television, and home video is growing two to three times faster than in the United States and is a strong driver of entertainment industry profits.

Look at the film industry as an example. With revenue pressure coming from an ever-increasing number of new releases and cost pressure coming from rising talent costs and advertising budgets, studios are relying more and more on ancillary revenue streams, including foreign distribution, to enhance traditional domestic box-office receipts. In fact, today the term ancillary is no longer valid because these markets are not an add-on but are in fact a vital part of the entertainment product lifecycle.

From the Internet to MTV, from British Sky Broadcasting to America Online and Europe Online, we are interconnected electronically as never before, and that phenomenon has now moved beyond the developed world to the parts of the world where development in telecommunications has only just begun—China, Southeast Asia, and Latin America.

Today, television can take young children across the globe before we give them permission to cross the street. And it is the young who are leading the charge. In such countries as India, Malaysia, Brazil, and Argentina, young and eager consumers of entertainment products are clamoring for their MTV (and even, on occasion, for their ESPN and CNN). These consumers are under 25, probably the first in their families to be able easily to afford such expenditures, and they love American entertainment—or, more to the point, American-style entertainment customized to their local tastes. These purchases were once the discretionary perks of the elite, but today, in many foreign markets, entertainment purchases are a staple of an enormous and growing middle class.

Technologies have effectively leveled the global playing field. Although cable, then fiber optics, then satellite distribution had to be laboriously pioneered in the United States, emerging markets can take immediate advantage of our latest and best advances.

We went from 13 channels to 35 channels to 66 channels and so on over many years, but people in Asia are going straight from no TV to multichannel television. In China, TV households have increased from 30 million in 1987 to 210 million today. In fact, the world's largest cable system is not in New York City or Los Angeles, where you might expect to find it, but in Shanghai.

So, the market is there and the distribution technology is, to a large extent, there, but an audience and a wire do not necessarily spell success.

The reality is: In many regions, government regulation has not kept pace with consumer demand or the onslaught of new entertainment products. There can be—and, in many cases, are—distribution bottlenecks that must be overcome.

The reality is: Although non-U.S. consumers are clamoring for more American entertainment, they are equally intent on maintaining their distinct cultural identities.

The reality is: In many global markets, copyright protection cannot be insured and piracy is rampant.

The reality is: In certain foreign markets, distribution monopolies are limiting the choices for consumers, and without distribution choice, overall growth will be limited.

None of these challenges is insurmountable, but none can be overlooked. Opportunity has its price.

New Technologies

What is *real* this decade is the sweep and impact of new technologies. The tremendous advances we have made technologically since the birth of the microprocessor only 25 years ago are hard to overrepresent. CD-ROM encyclopedias did not exist until recently. Now they outsell printed versions by the mile. Cellular phones until quite recently were luxury items. Now, they are practically given away to middle-class consumers.

And then there is the Internet. Almost 30 years after its inception, it has suddenly become *the* hot ticket and an integral part of our national discourse. Some 2,500 articles about the Internet appear each month in American newspapers.

The Internet is not part of the elusive future. It is here and now. And yet it still begs some major questions. What is its future? When will it be commercialized? When will it start generating revenues for companies, and what will be the source of those revenues? To use the old buzzword, what will be the killer application(s)?

The Internet offers immediate and direct access to tens of millions of consumers worldwide. It has doubled in size every year for the past six, with the World Wide Web growing at an even faster clip, from 2 million subscribers in 1994 to more than 10 million today. Still, when this past holiday season rolled around, those Internet cash registers were not bursting with consumer dollars. The retailing bonanza the Internet promised to spawn has so far failed to materialize. In fact, most surveys project that even by the year 2000, total sales of consumer goods and services on the Internet will barely top $1 billion. That is about half the size of today's annual market in blowdryers alone.

Today, the Internet is, for all intents and purposes, a marketing and promotional tool. *But the reality is*: it is the only medium—other than the telephone—that can simultaneously link consumers around the globe. No matter how you look at it, that spells opportunity. But getting from theoretical opportunity to a revenue-generating reality may be one of the greatest challenges our industry will face. The fundamental problem with the Internet is not anxiety over stolen credit cards; it is concern over the protection of copyrights. Currently, there is no safe commerce on the information highway. With more than 30 million people accessing the Internet in North America alone, there is a tremendous temptation to copy books, computer games, photographs, and songs into cyberspace. With the click of a mouse, copies can be made and distributed around the world. The original owner may never know about the copies, much less be paid for them.

For the media industry, which is founded on the creation of brands and copyrights, this lack of protection is, quite simply, throwing away money, and that, I can assure you, runs contrary to my nature. Both the media industry and the U.S. government have a vested interest in meeting this challenge head on. The United States is the world's largest creator, packager, and exporter of copyright material. We are, in essence, the world's primary idea factory. Intellectual property in the form of books, films, music, multimedia games, and educational products is fast becoming the currency in which our country trades. Indeed, intellectual property adds more value to our economy than any single manufacturing sector—more than aircraft, textiles, chemicals, or industrial machinery.

The Clinton administration has already taken a major step toward making commerce on the information highway safe by releasing a long-term Commerce Department study, which is the overture to legislation assuring that the protection of intellectual property keeps pace with technology. We look to Congress to keep abreast of this vital issue and take effective and far-sighted action. America's leadership in the information age depends on it.

The enormous challenge of effectively and safely exploiting new technologies is what is *real* this decade.

Company Power

The fourth key force, which is an outgrowth of the first three, is the need for size, scale, and sheer power in this new media landscape.

The companies that have the wherewithal and marketplace strength to push their legislative agendas today, to make the capital investments needed to expand globally this year, and to defend vigorously their creative content and brands in this digital decade are not the small upstarts of this world. They are companies with *gravitas*—market clout. Viacom recognized that advantage when it merged with Paramount and Blockbuster in 1994, and the headline-grabbing merger activity of the past year has only confirmed it.

The reality is: In a rapidly changing global entertainment world, being bigger and more powerful is essential to mitigate risks, create leverage, and keep the playing field from being dominated by adversarial gatekeepers. To be sure, other elements may be contributing to the current "dealmania" that has engulfed our industry. Some may be buying and selling in lieu of pursuing a clear-cut vision. Some may be looking at grabbing headlines, obtaining bragging rights about being the biggest, as if that were the end in itself. Still others—including Viacom—are recognizing that although bigger is not necessarily better, bigger is better than smaller. It is a matter of simple economics. To successfully open a movie these days can take upward of $100 million. The home video market—now 50 percent of entertainment industry revenues—requires increasingly large capital outlays in marketing and distribution. New media—which will see a lot of future growth—require significant up-front capital investments. In this sort of environment, big is good, and if properly managed and exploited, big is great.

Last year, consumers spent $150 billion on communications and entertainment products. Domestic spending alone is expected to reach nearly $200 billion by 1999, and the global marketplace shows every sign of growing. Success in this global media landscape will play out in the backyards of the big players. At the same time, there will still be plenty of opportunity for small, creative firms—particularly content providers—as these media giants define and open new markets.

Media Management

The media world as I see it is unpredictable, increasingly accessible, and ever evolving. Charting a course for success in this environment requires much more than cogent analysis. In the end, it also requires gut instinct.

A pilot study by the newly formed Entrepreneurial Research Consortium notes that although some 7 million American adults are trying to start businesses, as many as half will never actually open them. Something beyond raw number crunching is obviously involved in making a business work. Success also has nothing to do with luck. There is nothing haphazard about either starting a business or taking an existing company and transforming it into a larger, more competitive organization.

The key element in the equation is instinct. By this, I mean an ability to synthesize one's total experience with an analytic and rational mind. It is said that decisions reached by one's "gut" get attributed to intuition, but people lack the vocabulary for what they are really doing: using a sophisticated form of pattern recognition. One's gut instinct, I suppose, can be defined as a person's lifetime experience and the ability to synthesize that experience into the right decision at the right time.

The truly difficult decisions in business cannot be made on an accumulation of facts alone. Business success will always be determined by visionaries—people who can cull existing facts and historical knowledge to form an appreciation for what is likely to happen in the future and then act on it. Indeed, trying to foretell the future is the most difficult of all business actions and probably the most important. It can lead to management decisions that are both painful to make and troublesome to comprehend for many on the outside. In the end, you must trust your instinct, you must have faith in your vision for the future if you are to make the hard, but necessary, choices successful business requires.

About the Future

At the midpoint of the decade, it seems clear that the big, seamless digital tapestry hailed as just around the corner is at least a few years away, although some of the threads may already be apparent. It is also clear that the future depends upon what we do with those threads.

When you think about the future, think about the media pundits who were eulogizing the television network business. What is real is that today, two of those networks—ABC and CBS—are changing hands at values five times greater than they were valued in 1990. By the year 2000, I believe that there will be *five* major networks and that they will be among the most valuable media properties because of their singular ability to deliver to advertisers broad audiences in a fragmented world.

When you think about the future, think about the common wisdom that declared MTV a "fad" and dismissed Ted Turner's CNN as a money-losing fantasy. What is real is that today MTV is the largest and most successful cable network in the world, reaching nearly 270 million households and my competitors are lining up to launch one of those "money losing" cable news networks. I predict that by the year 2000 many more cable networks will be well established around the world, entertaining, informing, and even educating people in nearly 1 billion households from Bombay to Buenos Aires.

When you think about the future, think about pay-per-view forecasts that exploding revenues would top $780 million by 1995 and would quickly replace the videocassette and that the videocassette would devastate pay television. What is real is that pay-per-view generated only $470 million in revenues in 1995, and the number of VCRs on a worldwide basis has grown 43 percent in the past five years. What is also real is that technology is additive and that it cannot replace programming that is efficiently delivered and cost-effectively packaged under strong brand names such as HBO and Showtime. As I look ahead to the year 2000, I see home video and pay TV as still the only delivery vehicles attractive to the mass market.

When you think about the future, think about the fact that in 1990 foreign markets accounted for less than 45 percent of total theatrical motion picture revenues. What is real is that in less than five years, foreign market revenues increased to 52 percent of the total. This growth will be further accelerated by the build-out and refurbishment of theaters in Latin America, Europe, and Asia; soon to follow will be theaters in Eastern Europe, the former USSR, and China. As a result, I believe that foreign markets will account for up to 70–80 percent of total box-office revenues by the year 2000.

When you think about the future, think about the fact that Ted Turner started with a bankrupt billboard company in South Carolina; that Rupert Murdoch started with a single newspaper in Adelaide, Australia; and that John Malone spent his early days in media working opposite Bob Magnes. Think about where these men are today. Think about the fact that they are part of a small, core group of leaders who have continued to redefine the scope of the media industry, pushing the envelope to new edges. You know what these leaders have already accomplished; think about what they still have up their sleeves.

When you think about the future, think about the media industry landscape in 1990—the newly merged Capital Cities/ABC and Time Warner, Paramount Communications, NBC, CBS, Disney, Turner Broadcasting, TCI (Tele-Communications Inc.), MCA, Columbia, Sony, News Corp., Comcast, Bertelsmann, Maxwell Communications, MGM, Miramax, New Line Cinema, and Castle Rock Entertainment, to name a few. Today, there are about a dozen major players: Time Warner/Turner, Disney/Capital Cities, Viacom, NBC, TCI, Bertelsmann, Westinghouse/CBS, Sony, and News Corp. By the year 2000, there will be a handful of global media giants—some from this list and others yet to arrive, such as a combination of AT&T and Time Warner possibly called TW/AT&T or maybe TW/USWEST/AT&T or maybe Bell Atlantic and NYNEX called BYNEX. The concentration of power will be awesome. Who will be the major players when we reach the millennium?

Conclusion

No one can fully predict the future. What is real today, this year, and this decade is the following: We are operating in a far more competitive and global market these days, in which the intelligent deployment of technology, scale, and international reach and sheer commitment and intellectual capacity will drive success.

The companies that recognize that reality and capitalize on it will be the ones to watch.

Question and Answer Session

Sumner M. Redstone

Question: This industry is getting extremely competitive. How do you expect to keep your margins up?

Redstone: Competition is fine. In fact, in our particular case, most of the competition that is going to take place will be more to the benefit of the content provider. Most of the competition today is in distribution systems—direct broadcasts, telephone companies, and so on. That is to our advantage. Competition has never bothered Viacom. We have lived with it all the time and know how to address it—as long as the playing field is level. We also know how to level an unleveled playing field, if that is necessary.

Question: If bigger is better, do you have your eyes on future acquisitions?

Redstone: We are not going to overleverage the company, nor are we, having in mind the interest of all the stockholders, going to go for a massive dilution of our stockholders' interest. Today is the day for us. People forget what we have accomplished in less than two years. Biting off Paramount, Simon and Schuster, and Blockbuster has created an enormous company. We have enough to do and enough opportunity to increase our business without deal making. There may be a day when we will be opportunistic, but it is not today.

Question: Are there any big non-U.S. players in this industry?

Redstone: Well, there are Bertelsmann, CLT, Canal-Plus, and the Kirch Group in Germany. We are familiar with all of those people. In fact, we are going to Europe to meet with all of them because at some point we have to make a major sale of our programming library. Yes, there are non-U.S. companies, but they are not the same size as the companies here in the United States.

Question: Can you shed some light on the content versus distribution debate?

Redstone: In this industry, content is king; distribution depends on what is on it. The content providers are going to emerge as the big winners in a world in which distribution technologies are expanding. For that reason, we are concentrating on content, not distribution. On the other hand, Blockbuster is a major distribution system, and it is working well for us. It produces a lot of money. Its opportunities overseas cannot even be estimated. We are building stores all over the world. That is a distribution system, but we tend to think of distribution more in the context of what it can provide for content providers.

Question: What are the major risks in this industry?

Redstone: The risk would be not taking advantage of the opportunities that exist or not realizing the challenges, and in the case of our company, there is no chance of either taking place. All our businesses are very sound. Along the way, we may have shortfalls for a quarter o- two, but our businesses are doing extremely well and will do a lot better as we approach next year. One of the great risks that any company has is management, a risk that some of our competitors have today. What management brings to the business and the assets of a company makes a difference and can make that company a winner. Viacom has in-depth, diversified, talented, creative management. If a company cannot manage its people and the people are not working together as a team, then taking on more assets is a big risk.

Question: How will the cable and broadcasting market develop in Europe?

Redstone: Where cable is already part of the infrastructure and is already building, you are going to see cable. The big step forward is going to take place in direct broadcast. DirecTV is committed to going all over the world. This is not a small enterprise; it is General Motors. It has gone into direct broadcast here in the United States and knows what it is doing. For most places that do not already have cable, the question is: Why put it there? For what it costs, you can put up a satellite. All of the distribution systems will see some expansion, but direct broadcast is the name of the game, particularly in underdeveloped countries.

The Media Industry

The Regulatory Environment

George Reed-Dellinger
Vice President
HSBC Washington Analysis

> The Telecommunications Act of 1996 will significantly affect the media industry, with commensurate repercussions for the stocks in this sector. Although it will affect all major players, some will benefit more than others. Among the beneficiaries will be telephone companies and TV broadcasters. Less fortunate will be cable companies, newspapers, and wireless services.

The 104th Congress recently passed legislation that will turn 20 percent of the S&P 500 upside down. Laws, not technology, separate about eight industry submarkets, and the law is changing. Wall Street has done a generally poor job of analyzing Washington issues in general and this legislation in particular.

What occurs in Washington is likely to have a bigger impact on many stocks, particularly telemedia stocks, than the next quarter's earnings per share (EPS). The 1992 Cable Act turned the 1984 Cable Act upside down and reversed analyst and portfolio manager investment incentives when dealing with such stocks as Tele-Communications Inc. (TCI) and Time Warner. The same will probably happen in television with the elimination of financial interest and syndication rules (Fin-Syn). Deals among the major networks and television operators dominated the investment scenario beginning in the second half of 1995, and more are to come.

This presentation reviews the legislation and who I think the winners and losers are. It addresses some of the major regulatory issues that will be in front of investors during the next year, some antitrust issues, and some miscellaneous issues dealing with Time Warner, Turner Broadcasting System (TBS), and Microsoft. I also comment on spectrum, an issue that cuts across almost all industry lines.

Telecommunications Legislation

Legislation has been brewing in Washington since the 1934 Federal Communications Act passed. Once a bill is passed, people want to change it or find something that was overlooked. Congress will probably have to pass a technical-correction bill down the road to take care of the mess the Telecommunications Act of 1996 creates.

This legislation was driven by a turf fight between Congress and the courts. The power to set telecommunications authority rests constitutionally with Congress, but that authority was ceded to the courts for more than 15 years. Telecommunications authority since the 1982 consent decree in the Bell system and the 1984 divestiture has been driven by one federal court represented by Judge Harold Green, who was appointed for life. In 1993, courts found unconstitutional the 1984 Cable Act provision precluding telephone companies from offering their subscribers video service. This ruling left a huge void in regulatory policy.

Several years ago, a large wave of megamergers took place in the telemedia industry—Bell Atlantic, TCI, Time Warner, U S West, AT&T, McCaw Cellular Communications (now AT&T Wireless), British Telecommunications, MCI—and a cry went up in Congress to do something. The 1996 act is a response to the merger mania. It offers many election-year-friendly characteristics, and Congress was desperate to pass anything. The average voter is unlikely to be affected by this act in any meaningful fashion for years, but Congress will be able to take credit for enacting legislation.

Winners and Losers

The Wall Street wisdom is wrong in thinking this act is a zero-sum game with winners matched by losers. It is a Christmas tree bill: It has something in it for almost every industry. Investors will need to determine who gets what benefit, who gives up more than expected, who gets more than expected, and what has been discounted in the share prices.

Cable Companies

Since 1991, I have been bearish on the cable television industry, and this legislation gives me no reason to change my opinion. Expectations for the companies' rates being deregulated were too ambitious. The original language would have deregulated advertising-supported rates in 1997, but that timing is too close to fall elections. Deregulation will not take place until 1999. The cable spokesman will downplay the disappointment and say, "We have enough flexibility within the existing Federal Communications Commission (FCC) cable rules. Our real goal was not rate deregulation but to open up opportunities within the telephone market."

Moreover, the 1996 legislation does not deal with some 20 other provisions that were found in the 1992 Cable Act. **Table 1** outlines what most Wall Street analysts overlook, including "must carry" service requirements, accounting practices, and program ownership limits. No particular provision in and of itself is bearish, but when added up, the act is messy. The 1992 Cable Act turned a cable operator into nothing more than a common carrier, rate-of-return, regulated utility distributing somebody else's programming into a market that was becoming increasingly competitive.

I am not as bearish on vertically integrated companies such as Time Warner and TCI. Their programming and distribution capabilities—and the synergies that they derive—are substantial. The pure cable operator, standing alone, should not command a multiple premium to that of a telephone company. Also, some provisions of the 1996 legislation would preclude telephone or cable companies from taking over one another inside their own service territories. Deregulation could occur more quickly, but the company must demonstrate that competition exists. After the 1992 act, cable systems moved from being an unregulated monopoly in a growth market into regulated competitors that have to compete with one hand tied behind their backs, a predicament like AT&T's after the 1984 breakup. Cable operators in the future will be flipped out of the regulatory frying pan into the competitive skillet. Neither of these scenarios is as comfortable as the one the cable industry enjoyed prior to the 1992 act. In sum, the cable operators will not be the beneficiaries of a large deregulatory rate windfall. The legislation does not cure their problems.

The new legislation, however, has tilted my view in favor of the investment prospects confronting the television broadcasters, and investors will probably get more bang for the buck if they look at the smaller independent TV stations that could be taken over.

Telephone Companies

The new act will open up the telephone local market to all comers, but no recent tilt in the language would serve to offset the effect of having cable rate deregulation pushed out for two years, which will disappoint cash flow projections. Cable

Table 1. 1992 Cable Act

Regulation	Result	Adverse Impact
Rate regulation	17+% September cut	Cash flow
Municipal authority		Regulatory costs/lags
Competitive access to programming		Competition/litigation
"Must carry"	Upheld	Cash flow
"Retransmission consent"	Upheld	Cash flow
Service standards		Cash flow
3-year anti-trafficking		Liquidity
Customer wire sales option		Competition
Channel ownership limit	40%	Growth
Subscriber ownership limit	Struck down	Growth
Advertising channels	Inquiry	Cash flow
DBS (satellite) obligations	Struck down	Competition
Equipment compatibility		Cash flow
Obscenity requirements	Struck down	Cash flow
Sports migration study		Growth
Equal opportunity standards		Cash flow
Municipal legal liability limits		Litigation
Franchise renewal		Competition

Source: HSBC Washington Analysis.

does not have many friends in Washington. The few friends it has feel sorry for cable companies and worry that in head-to-head competition, the phone companies will smash them.

My investment themes suggest that AT&T and MCI are beneficiaries, not victims, of the bill. The stocks of these two companies have been disproportionately beaten down because of exaggerated and misplaced legislative risk. The Bell companies are not the big winners that the *Wall Street Journal* claims they are, and they are subject to more risk than investors imagine. The Bell companies' stocks have not appreciated much. The broadcasters' stocks were spiked upward by the actions industry players have taken starting midyear 1995, when a raft of takeovers took place within the broadcasting industry.

Television Broadcasters

TV broadcasters have benefited significantly from changes in regulatory events during the past several years. They will be able to undergo a fundamental, positive change in their secular fundamentals. The 1992 Cable Act handicapped their cable industry competitors. It also provided the broadcasters with some benefits that do not show up on a financial sheet—for example, retransmission consent provisions, which helped change the TV operators' bargaining position with cable. The expiration of the financial interest and syndication rules has had a major impact on how the chief executives of these companies look at the TV broadcast industry. These Fin-Syn rules had limited the networks' participation in the lucrative downstream portion of the syndication markets since 1970 and prevented them from controlling their programming costs and from merging with Hollywood studios.

The demise of Fin-Syn, the handicaps accruing to the cable industry, and the changes proposed by this legislation make the TV broadcasters the largest net large-cap beneficiaries of this act. They do not have to give up a lot.

The receipt of a second TV channel is causing some controversy. Currently, this issue is only an FCC proposal. To codify the receipt of such a channel, as the new act will do, would be positive. Use of that channel will be allowed for nonbroadcast purposes such as paging or one-way information downloading. This spectrum flexibility, as such use is called, offers the opportunity to generate a second or third revenue stream and possibly wean the broadcasters off 70 years of dependency on the vagaries of advertising. The flexibility probably will not give the broadcasters enough capacity to provide two-way mobile voice services in competition with cellular, but it does not take much bandwidth to offer a paging service or a one-way information downloading service that could eliminate all the wires in offices where people are trying to receive their Bloomberg input, their quote input, their Bridge input, and so forth.

Another benefit broadcasters will receive from this legislation is the elimination of the network 12-station ownership limit. The 25 percent associated cap on nationwide viewership will be expanded to 35 percent. This expansion should provide scale economies. Broadcasters can be in a much stronger bargaining position with advertisers when they have 35 percent market reach, not 25 percent. By picking up more stations, broadcasters can lay off much of the production and overhead costs that have been borne by 12 stations. This provision allows the networks to take greater advantage of the benefits accruing from the elimination of Fin-Syn. These new capabilities will probably feed a takeover frenzy; adding a 13th station improves the value of the network, and the 13th station, by being added to the network, also has its value enhanced.

How the other provisions of the act will be implemented is uncertain. Could a TV operator own two stations in a given city? Some provisions allow a network to own a cable operator. Also important to broadcasters is the right to extend license renewal out to eight years, and they will not be held hostage as often by those who challenge renewal in the hope of being bought off.

The sum of these benefits—a second revenue stream, scale economies, takeover frenzies—does not include the potential value of the companies' spectrum on their balance sheets. The broadcasters look cheap on a "price per population" valuation. Prices per pop are not equally comparable between cellular and paging and between microwave and satellite, not to mention entertainment and TV broadcasts. Some ambitious sell-side analyst will attempt to say, however, that CBS is selling at a couple bucks a pop. The controversial issue is going to be the spectrum they are supposed to get from the FCC. Spectrum is not going to be a giveaway, however. The issue of high-definition television has been on the table for more than a decade. The new spectrum is a transitional way to move from analog television to digital television. Broadcasters know they will eventually have to give the existing channel back. They probably had their fingers crossed up until about a year or two ago, thinking they would delay the inevitable.

Once the government smells the fruit of raising revenue from spectrum, heaven help us all, because selling spectrum is viewed as the cure for the budget deficit. I would rather sell Wyoming or Montana. The political net result will not cause a large, incremental hit on the cost of spectrum to the broadcasters. If broadcasters use the spectrum for nonbroadcast purposes, however, provisions in the act would have the FCC hit them with a fee on a prorated basis that would be equivalent to what, say, a paging service operator might have paid for equivalent spectrum capacity in the free markets.

The broadcasters also have to retrofit their transmission towers and process new programming. Advertisers may not pay up for high-definition television. Being able to digitize a signal offers the opportunities of multiple channels, clearly a good opportunity for broadcasters, but to think that spectrum is a giveaway is wrong.

The whole issue will be settled in a revenue-raising measure. Auctioning off the new channel would be money out of the broadcasters' pockets. Returning the existing analog channel for the government to auction off is already in the cards; the question is when. The hope is that by the time it is auctioned off, the transition to digital would have already been made. Who knows what will happen in 10 years? The broadcasters may or may not have to lay out money if they want to participate in recapturing a second existing analog channel that has already been destined to be given back to the government anyway. The return of the existing analog channel in, say, 10 years is an entirely different animal; about 20 percent of the United States would still have old televisions that could not receive a broadcast in digital format.

All these benefits will accrue to the networks, but Chris-Craft Industries, Tribune Company, or A.H. Belo Corporation might be better values because they may offer the critical mass for potential fifth or sixth networks. They also represent lucrative stations that the existing networks could bid for, once given permission.

Newspaper Publishers

Newspapers are included in telemedia, but they have been rather quiet. For the past 10 years, they have feared that their advertising, classified ads, and want ads would be siphoned away by electronic yellow pages. For example, if it is snowing, someone with a personal computer could find out where a shovel could be purchased, order that shovel by phone, and have it delivered. Anything that siphons away business from a limited advertising market to an electronic format is a threat. The newspapers are listened to. Every politician can open up a desk and pull out an editorial in which he or she was slammed by the local newspaper. Newspapers have several years of protection before the Bell companies can freely offer their electronic yellow pages format. The newspapers are also being picked up, escorted, and subsidized to make sure that they get on the electronic information superhighway.

Related Industries

Hollywood studios are not directly affected by the act, but the legislation cuts across all communications lines. By allowing phone companies to deliver a video service quickly and easily, this act can only enhance the secular demand for a product with content.

Telecommunications equipment companies such as General Instrument Corporation and Scientific-Atlanta Incorporated also are not directly affected by the act. If, however, the act breaks down the barriers that separate the approximately eight telemedia industries, thereby allowing TV broadcasters to offer paging services and cable operators to offer telephony services, then there will be an upward spike in telemedia equipment demand. The tech investors have recognized this potential during the past year. The equipment companies were probably a no-brainer for investors who could not figure out exactly what the act would do.

The Bell Companies

The Bell companies may be better off in the courts than in Congress. The courts have been granting exceptions to the consent decree. The odds are that future courts will be more sympathetic to a Bell company. The reason is that the jurists are likely to have been appointed by the Reagan or Bush administration and would like to see the government out of the Bell companies' hair.

Congress does not give away gifts for free. The Bell companies will have to give up a great deal more than people think. Their stocks could be bought for reasons—such as portfolio rotation, defensiveness, or yield—but buying on the belief that they will get a big legislative win is mistaken. The Bell companies will not have to open up their local monopolies. After 11 years, the Bell companies, in a portfolio sense, have faced nothing but upside gain. Investors thought that if the companies could get past Judge Green, they could to go into the promised land of long distance. Although the probability of such a development was not high, the risk was only in one direction—upside gain. Now, they have to go through the process of opening their markets to competitors, changing their infrastructure, and demonstrating that they face some competition before they have the right to go into long distance. If they go into long distance, they will be shackled by regulatory safeguards that might handicap any eventual success they may have.

The independents—such as Sprint, Century Telephone Enterprises, and GTE—may face an even worse scenario. Independents can go into long distance now, and they will not get any benefits, but they will all have to open their local telephone monopolies.

AT&T and MCI will not be the victims that the *Wall Street Journal* and many market forecasters believe. The portion of this act that requires the regional Bell operating companies (RBOCs) to open their monopoly first will probably drive down access charges rapidly. AT&T and MCI will realize billions of dollars of access charge savings before the Bells get any meaningful entry into long distance. NYNEX has been everybody's whipping boy because of its exposure to competition. The legislation would let NYNEX be the first out of the gate among the Bells to offer local and long-distance service and possibly put NYNEX in a league to do that nationwide. The game seems to be a one-shop nationwide service provider. NYNEX and possibly Ameritech will be the leaders there, and if I had to buy a Bell operating company, it would probably be one of those two companies. The companies resisting the act the most are BellSouth and U S West.

Wireless

We have entered a bear market in cellular values. I would avoid AirTouch Communications, Nextel Communications, and internationally, Vodafone Group PLC. They are the pure holders of wireless licenses. The government controls 40 percent of all the radio frequencies. The balance between supply and demand has been static all of our lifetime. The government now plans to take spectrum away from itself and give it to private industry. When the supply of a good increases, its value decreases. The government is not giving the spectrum away for free, however. It will tax it or place a user's fee on it. Can this tax be passed along to end users? If so, it will probably decrease the elasticity of demand; if not, it will hurt margins.

Many other rule changes allow interindustry and intraindustry mobile communications competition. Sprint is in the forefront of personal communications service (PCS) and is attacking the existing cellular operators. The ensuing rate war will not fit the trend that most of the more bullish analysts would lead people to expect.

With this act, TV broadcasters might be viewed as hot on the heels of PCS and specialized mobile radio (SMR) by offering some of their spectrum for mobile radio communications services. Put on top of that the advent of digital technology replacing analog technology, and the result is a quantum increase in capacity. The only impact that development can have on rates is downward by making demand more elastic.

Question and Answer Session

George Reed-Dellinger

Question: In your bearish comments on the cable companies, you did not mention potential new revenue sources such as cable modems. Do such products have the potential to change your outlook if the technology works?

Reed-Dellinger: I have been waiting for switches to be added, for two-way interactivity, and for an increase in channels, but I am not holding my breath. My problem with cable is that it has a large, attractive pipeline—broadband. That capacity is an advantage over the phone companies, but it is a primitive system. It is largely one-way. The cable companies lack switching capability, which is the ability of the telephone network to send a signal across the street to your neighbor or across the country. I am not sure a modem will change the equation in the long term. The cable companies will have to add a new dimension to their plants—not merely replace a dimension the way the phone companies have to replace narrow band with broadband, but add a whole layer of assets—and they have to do that with the worst credit rating in the industry. Capital is the problem, not technology. Even though modems cost money, switches cost more money, and upgrading service and two-way voice grade interactivity costs a great deal of money.

Question: You insist that cable is a loser and competitive access providers (CAPs) are winners. Where do you place the cable operators who have aligned themselves with MFS Communications and Sprint?

Reed-Dellinger: I do not consider cable a loser, but it is not going to get the big win that the more bullish cable analysts might have projected. It will not get the win that lifted some of the prices for the cable stocks during the past year. The 1996 act was written so that MFS Communications would succeed. If Congress wants this act to be effective, then the CAPs have to lift themselves from their *de minimis* revenues of $500 million. Any alliance that cable could have with the CAPs would be positive. I would be careful about what you are paying, who will get control, and who will get the bulk of the value added from the deal. The Bells are about 7 percent of the S&P 500. There is no real alternative to the CAPs for investors to play, so it is probably going to be a seller's market for CAP stocks.

Question: What do you expect the FCC's role would be going forward?

Reed-Dellinger: The FCC will have to put in place a minimum of 80 separate rule makings to effectuate the 1996 act. The FCC rule-making process is as follows: It issues a notice of proposal or a notice of inquiry; then, it announces a final order, assuming there is not a second notice of proposal; after a final order (which is not final) comes a petition for reconsideration that could overturn the final order; this petition is sent to the court, and if the lower court does not send it back to the FCC, the appellate court might.

Question: Will the FCC enact a cleanup bill for Congress?

Reed-Dellinger: Some of the 1996 act, such as the definition of a competitor, is purposely left unclear. Bells do not get into long distance until they have competitors. Universal service is the large pool that subsidizes cheap telephone rates to people in the rural areas. Universal service is politically sensitive because rural senators and rural members of Congress have a disproportionate weight on the judicial and commerce committees. Universal service is one big can of worms. There have to be more new services, and each new service has to be unbundled into various subelements. All of them have to have a number—a tariff, a dollar, a per minute rate, a flat rate—and all of those numbers are artificial points between two artificial estimates, all of which are decided on a political basis by a regulator. So, universal service is one of those services that overlaps with every other service that will be offered. Separate bills will be required to determine what the universal service fund is and what the other unknown pieces of confusion are that this legislation has caused. The FCC and the states will be in the middle of it. Every Bell company has to go through a state regulator to get certification that it has implemented the market-opening, procompetitive checklist that the legislation mandates.

Question: Focusing on broadcasters, what is your outlook for radio?

Reed-Dellinger: The FCC has already acted on radio. Radio operators get nowhere near the benefits that accrue to the TV broadcasters. The FCC has already raised the station-ownership limits that accrue to radio. Radio does not get spectrum flexibility or a second free channel. The run-up in radio stocks might have been a no-brainer and easy, but the benefits accruing to TV broadcasters might not be easy to value fully. I do not think the benefits of radio come close to those that accrue to a TV broadcaster, yet the stocks have taken off.

Question: Is consolidation likely for RBOCs? If so, who are the most likely participants?

Reed-Dellinger: Nothing in the consent decree mandates that there be seven Bell companies. AT&T picked that number because it did not want to deal with one monolithic monopsonist that would control all of AT&T's supply of incoming and outgoing telephone calls. In some respects, the legislation complicates takeovers. For example, if NYNEX is first out of the gate to offer long distance in New York, why would it want to team with Bell Atlantic if Bell Atlantic were precluded from being in the long-distance business? One scenario is that the Pacific Telesis Group combines with US West to serve the Pacific Rim, SBC Communications teams with BellSouth to serve the Spanish-speaking areas to the south, and Bell Atlantic and Ameritech combine, which leaves NYNEX alone. The 1996 act will complicate matters about who merges with whom, but it opens some other interesting merger opportunities. The AT&T consent decree currently precludes it from owning a Bell company asset. When AT&T bid for McCaw Cellular Communications and McCaw shared cellular ownership interests with a Bell operating company, Judge Green had to get involved. That portion of the decree is eliminated, so this act enhances the chances of AT&T taking over a Bell company and a Bell company asset.

Question: AT&T is about to break up. Which of the new companies to be spun off will be the largest beneficiaries?

Reed-Dellinger: The manufacturing arm. I expect that equipment stocks will go up and that AT&T will spin off its manufacturing arm. A significant bias has been present among Bell companies, the largest purchasers of equipment in the United States, not to buy equipment from a vertically integrated AT&T/Western Electric because they view that combination as their primary competitor. Western Electric will get more orders, not only from the telemedia universe but from the Bell companies specifically.

A provision in the house bill, which was stricken from the unified bill, would have made a Bell company pass the open market checklist in every state before it could get into the manufacturing business. Currently, I think it allows a Bell company in New York to get into the manufacturing business in New York if the Bell company in New York could offer long-distance services in New York. No doubt, the final legislation will help the Western Electric arm that has not been named yet but that is due for an IPO at the end of this quarter.

Question: How is the legislation evolving to allow foreign long-distance companies to penetrate the U.S. market?

Reed-Dellinger: Both houses of Congress passed bills that would have promoted reciprocal increases in limits on foreign ownership of U.S. broadcast licenses. Originally, media companies, such as Fox Broadcasting, and long-distance companies—such as MCI, which is owned by British Telecommunications—would have benefited from increases in foreign-ownership ceilings. Subsequently, only common carrier communications companies could have their foreign-ownership ceilings increased. Increased foreign ownership dropped off the negotiating table. The broadcasters had too many other issues they wanted to pursue, and they did not put a premium on having Rupert Murdoch let off the hook with respect to foreign-ownership ceilings. On December 20, 1995, because of the leverage Senator Ernest F. Hollings (D-SC) has in the Senate and because of the leverage the Senate has over the Congress and the fact that the White House is controlled by a Democrat that now might listen to Senator Hollings, the increased foreign-ownership ceilings were dropped out of the bill, much to the displeasure of Congressman Michael Oxley (R-OH). Currently, the Congress is trying to say that increased foreign ownership would be brought up and addressed in a separate piece of legislation. They are not going to pass a separate piece of legislation in 1996; they may never do it. Currently, the FCC has the authority to grant an increase in the 25 percent foreign-ownership limit on a case-by-case basis. It has a proceeding going forward that would expand that case-by-case waiver to a more generic, broad, applicable rule. One of the disappointments is that the United States is still restrictive on opening up networks to foreign owners.

Question: Will there be a telecom bill every year?

Reed-Dellinger: There will be a bill every year but not a law every year. A bill has been passed every year since 1934. A technical-correction bill will probably be passed in 1997.

The Media in 2005

Dennis H. Leibowitz
Senior Vice President, Research
Donaldson, Lufkin & Jenrette

> In the next century, the media industry will be affected by regulation, technological change, internationalization, and structural changes that are taking place today. Regulatory changes will lead to consolidation, and giant conglomerates will dominate the industry. Consolidation will lead to shifts in market shares. The big winners are likely to be the software producers, the entertainment companies, and the companies that produce services that will now, because of these vast changes, have multiple buyers.

The scenario for the media and communications business in the year 2005 is in a very active stage of formation. The companies that will be the giants 10 years from now are putting the pieces together today in a fairly tumultuous environment. The changes underway in regulation, technology, internationalization, consolidation and diversification, and markets will affect the future of the industry. An additional factor that will determine the fate of the media industry is the investment opportunities, particularly the strength in the stock market.

Regulation

The recent trend in regulation is to open all markets to competition. Monopolies will not exist in the future. All the media companies are positioning themselves to be able to compete in this new environment. The purpose of this governmental policy is to try to stimulate the electronic, or information, superhighway. Because competition will open up, the drive toward vertical and horizontal integration, which the regulations permit now, is tremendous. The theory is that fewer safeguards are needed if the environment is more competitive, and the players need more financial flexibility so that they can invest billions of dollars to upgrade in order to compete in the future.

Greater concentration is under way in this industry, depending on the new communications legislation. For example, broadcast ownership rules will allow one company to own more than one station and cross-ownership among various media.

What had been the historical tendency toward separate ownership in order to safeguard against too much media concentration in too few hands is in the process of being reversed. Television networks were considered dominant and potentially anticompetitive in the early 1970s, but now the financial interest syndication rules that prevented networks from consolidating have been lifted.

The removal of those same rules also permits the networks to be programmers and distributors. Companies such as Warner Bros. and Paramount fear loss of programming business from their traditional clients and are starting up new networks. The merger of Walt Disney Company and Capital Cities/ABC is a further integration of programming and distribution, using the Disney product, the ABC network, and the worldwide resources of ESPN. The Time Warner/Turner Broadcasting System arrangement allows distribution of films by Turner through the Warner Bros. distribution organization, which needs no extra overhead to distribute Turner's films. Similarly, the cartoon production capabilities at Warner Bros. are used on the Cartoon Network by Turner and others on a national and international basis.

The main accomplishment of the Telecommunications Act of 1996 is to open up competition—specifically, opening up the telephone market, which is the biggest single communications market, to include competition by cable operators. In turn, the video market and cable market, among others, will be open for play to the telephone companies. The telephone business is four and a half times larger than the cable sector; if each gets an equal share of the other's businesses, the cable operators would stand to gain more than the telephone companies. Cable operators also have less rebuilding to do than the telephone companies before they can get into the business. Cable operators' investment is heavily variable, meaning that the biggest investment they would have to make to get into the telephone business would be in a box outside of the house that would split the incoming signals between those going to the telephone and those going to the television or computer. This investment will vary with subscriber demands. The other major category of interest within the legislation is competition among the telephone companies (i.e., between the long-distance carriers and the local-exchange carriers).

Technology

After regulation, the next most important factor influencing this industry is technology. The advent of digital technology and the use of compression to allow multiple channels within the same spectrum space that used to carry only one will make available hundreds of channels to the average consumer. It also opens up interactive service possibilities for a number of uses such as video-on-demand and transaction services. Currently, the direct broadcast satellite (DBS) industry has an advantage because its product is digital and is proving to be very popular with subscribers. This demand for DBS is accelerating the need for the competitors, primarily the cable industry, to make massive investments in plant and digital boxes in order to compete.

Another important technological change is the rapid rollout of personal computers and the use of online services. This demand provides a niche opportunity for the cable industry, which has a window right now vis-à-vis the telephone companies in that the bandwidth of their coaxial cable is substantially greater than that of the telephone companies' twisted-pair copper wire. The cable industry is developing modems that will allow speeds 1,000 times faster than the traditional telephone delivery of online services and other computer information. This capability will be one of the driving forces of new business for the cable industry.

All of these developments will provide new revenues for a number of cable industry players in the form of online, pay-per-view, and other such services and for the information providers, whether software providers, publishers, or movie or television producers.

Internationalization

U.S. companies are now investing overseas, and to a lesser extent, the converse is also true, depending somewhat on liberalization of foreign-ownership regulations. The pressure in the United States is to undo some of the restrictions to the extent that other countries reciprocate. International markets provide new outlets for domestic products, often at a very cheap entry price. For example, Viacom and others can produce programs such as MTV—the appeal of which is not limited to English-speaking countries—for a relatively nominal price.

The MTV format has been very successful and is a source of higher growth internationally than domestically, which is a more mature market. The same goes for a production such as CNN. Also, the ability to buy product on a worldwide basis offers economies of scale. For example, News Corp. bought rugby rights for South Africa, India, and Australia that it will parlay to all countries to whom that product is attractive.

Consolidation and Diversification

From a practical standpoint, the stock market's main effect on the media industry is to have allowed companies to make acquisitions in exchange for stock rather than cash. For example, the Time Warner/Turner deal is a multibillion dollar merger that was only feasible, given the leverage of Time Warner, because it was a stock deal.

All of these changes are leading the industry toward offering a national, branded, bundled package of services for which discounts are offered to those who take multiple services. One company would offer cable service, long-distance service, local telephony, wireless telephony, computer services, and so forth. Customers would get discounts if they take more than one service. For example, the United Kingdom is currently the only country that permits a cable operator to offer telephone service. The cable companies offer a 15–20 percent discount to British Telecommunications' rates because many people who get cable also get telephone service from the cable company.

The proposed merger between Tele-Communications Inc. (TCI) and Bell Atlantic was the first domestic attempt at fulfilling this vision of combining cable and telephone services. Bell Atlantic's vision was to offer a national service with TCI representing the cable distribution on a national basis. They would have supplemented local telephony through cable in markets in which they did not have a presence themselves. The Telecommunications Act allows the local-exchange carriers into the long-distance business. Bell Atlantic is already into wireless service in a joint venture with NYNEX Corporation, and it hopes to expand into a bigger joint venture in personal communications service (PCS) and the newer cellular wireless business, which is under auction now. This joint venture would have included NYNEX, Bell Atlantic, AirTouch Communications, and U S West. Although the Bell Atlantic/TCI deal fell through, the idea has continued. The difference between then and now is that, now, the companies do not need to buy everything. They can resell. MCI Communications Corporation has used this strategy with respect to a number of the wireless services, but the company has to have all the pieces available to offer.

Another example is the joint venture between Sprint on the long-distance telephone side and a combination of cable companies—TCI, Cox Communications, and Comcast Corporation—that got together under the Sprint Telecommunications venture. This consortium has bid on wireless telephone licenses, and it is selling Sprint long-distance phone service through the cable companies. In turn, Sprint will offer entertainment services. When the law allows, that arrangement will be the vehicle for the cable operators, with the Sprint brand name on a national basis, to offer local telephony as well as cable. This agreement is an example of a national consortium that will offer a bundle of various products for discounts to other operators that take more than one product.

AT&T recently announced that it is going to invest in the services of DirecTV, the first and largest DBS operator, at a very high imputed value. DBS is only one slice of the pie. From AT&T's standpoint, this agreement, which is not mutually exclusive, leaves it open to make a similar deal in the cable industry. Rumors have been rampant that AT&T may join with Time Warner (which is already in a joint venture with U S West), and perhaps Continental Cablevision, to form an alliance that is the contra-attempt to the TCI/Sprint alliance.

MCI joined with News Corp. to place the winning bid in the recent auction of a DBS system. News Corp., with inputs in all of the sectors except the ownership of cable systems, is currently the best prototype of how the telecommunications industry is going to develop. It owns 20th Century Fox and *TV Guide*. It controls British Sky Broadcasting Group (BSkyB), the DBS operator in the United Kingdom; it is an investor in a DBS operator in Latin America; it has a joint venture with MCI in online services and in the DBS business; and it owns Star TV, which provides DBS services throughout Asia.

Bell Atlantic and NYNEX are jointly marketing their services and have taken control of a wireless cable company that is offering microwave entertainment—that is, the same services offered by cable but on a wireless basis—for the entire mid-Atlantic and northeast regions. They are buying the facilities of CAI Wireless Systems and using those licenses to do wireless cable in such major markets as New York, Philadelphia, Boston, Baltimore, Pittsburgh, and Washington, D.C. This action—a stop-gap measure in an effort to obtain a subscriber base while the companies wait for their own networks to become ready—is an admission that the telephone companies, which had announced bright plans to compete in video when the law allows, are far behind their own timetables. Current speculation predicts that Bell Atlantic and NYNEX will not only operate a joint venture but will eventually merge with each other and be the first of what may be more than one regional Bell operating company (RBOC) merger. Certainly, if AT&T, U S West, and Time Warner get together, the modified final judgment or a change in the regulations would be required. All these combinations are contingent upon or have been fed by changes in regulation.

The computer software companies are also getting into the act. Microsoft was involved in a purported joint venture with MCI in the online services business. MCI already has an arrangement with News Corp., which represents a little cannibalism on MCI's part. TCI is an investor in the Microsoft Network. Microsoft is also an investor in the paging and wireless businesses through investments in such companies as PageNet (Paging Network) and M-Tel (Mobile Telecommunications Technology).

Everyone is putting the pieces together for this vision of giant conglomerates that will come into existence as we get on the road to 2005. Consolidation in all of these businesses will put more power in fewer hands. The percentage of cable subscribers served by systems controlled by the top five operators will probably rise to about 80 percent or more within a few years because companies that are on a free-standing basis will find that competing as stand-alone operators against the giants will be increasingly difficult. The giants will be able to underprice and outpromote the smaller operators, and they will have a much bigger base over which to amortize their costs. They will be able to underprice in one area because they will make it up in another, if they get the volumes through discounting and packaging. That kind of pressure is what is

The Media Industry

speeding the consolidation in businesses such as the cable and programming industries and the television networks. Consolidation and mergers are occurring in these areas because the companies have concluded that they cannot operate individually without being crushed by consolidated competitors.

Tomorrow's Markets

Consolidation will lead to market share shifts. Among the future services that will be offered, some will be shifts of existing products to new people (market share shifts), but some will be new products that do not exist now. Of course, the market share of existing products might grow. On the first score, some of the $90 billion telephone business will be diverted to cable operators or long-distance players. The cable industry will lose some market share to DBS, MMDS (microwave or wireless cable), and eventually to the telephone companies. The video store chains will lose share as pay-per-view and video-on-demand services are offered on cable, DBS, or other outlets. The video game cartridge business will compete with interactive games provided by such services as the Sega Channel.

The online services are just starting. Cable modems that will allow transmission rates much faster than those of phone lines will be available soon. That is one product for which tests show an overwhelming demand, and this market should be attractive overall because of the growth of personal computers, online services, and Internet access.

Video-on-demand is one of the big hopes, but it is a two-stage process. Near video-on-demand is available now. DirecTV, for example, offers 50 channels of pay-per-view with a hit movie starting every 15 minutes. At a later stage of development, when the equipment has been put in place, true video-on-demand—viewers getting what they want when they want it—will exist. Viewers will be able to ask for a movie at 8:04 p.m. and get it at 8:04 p.m. They will also be able to use all the basic VCR commands: stop, pause, fast forward, and rewind. At that point, virtual dedicated lines will be in place. In fact, people have talked about the concept of channels disappearing. An ABC or NBC will survive, but viewers will have electronic "pipes" coming into their houses and will determine what they want to go over those pipes.

The interactive market is also new. Interactive banking (telemetry) might be conducted like meter reading, for which the utilities themselves pay. Banks might find it worth the costs to do the same. Shopping on an interactive basis may displace the traditional catalog and television shopping channels. Interactive advertising is the ability to have coupons distributed and printed through machines attached to the television.

The market itself can also expand. For example, cable penetration is 65 percent in this country, but it is 85 percent in Canada and 95 percent in Holland. In Holland, one reason for cable's popularity is that it costs only $7 a month. One reason that we think that cable's loss of market share does not necessarily mean loss of customers is that the marketplace can expand. We forecast that cable, which has shown increasing subscriber growth in the past two years despite the entry of DBS, will flatten out in subscriber growth and that more of its growth will come from new services. The effect of DBS, MMDS, and telephone company video competition will be to expand the marketplace, not simply to cannibalize the existing companies.

Consumer services are going in three directions: television, personal computer, and telephone. Television services will all convert to digital in the next few years and probably a wide-screen version once television broadcasting is uniformly digital in the aspect ratio—that is, the visual format seen in movie theaters. Several of these television services also have applications for the personal computer platform. Interactive services could be provided for either television or computer, and some functions would be better suited for computers. The consumer will be in active control and will have dedicated lines, like telephone lines now, for delivering a variety of services on demand.

Investment Opportunities

From a stock market standpoint, the winners are the software producers, the entertainment companies, and the companies that produce services that will have multiple buyers instead of one—a very attractive combination. The relationship is synergistic for these companies, because they never had competing demands for their product before and they are not subject to the technology risks that others, such as the cable companies, face.

Pay television was a fairly mature category for a while, but it has shown good growth in the past couple of years. The DBS market has been wonderful for such companies because DBS is a new market, and the pay TV producers have gotten very attractive prices from the DBS operators buying the product.

The telephone companies have the most to lose. Market share gains are more likely to be at their expense than in their favor, as compared with some of the other media. They are hoping that the opportunities in the long-distance sector, with its relatively high margins, will more than make up for their loss of market share elsewhere. Also, they have their own new opportunities in video and other services.

The cable industry is too close to call. Cable stocks have been fairly poor performers for a while now. Initially, they suffered from two rounds of very drastic rate cuts from which they are only now recovering. Going forward, the problem has been the market's concern over how the competitive environment shakes out. What investors have determined for the short term is that they have not decided whether they would win or lose in cable stocks, so they do not want to play right now. To some extent, the same is true in wireless. Cable has more to gain than lose. Its largest potential opportunity is a combination of revenue streams from telephony. Cable modems are the nearest opportunity; video-on-demand and interactive services will mean an escalation of revenue per subscriber and profitability, even though cable's market share in the total pie will probably go down.

Conclusion

The pieces of the future media industry are being assembled today. The consensus is that a few giant conglomerates will offer multiple services at discounted prices. Companies that are not part of these giant conglomerates are going to get crushed. Consumers will gain new services, cheaper prices, and better quality through new technology.

Question and Answer Session

Dennis H. Leibowitz

Question: What kind of switching equipment is needed on the other side of a cable modem? How will the cable companies finance this expansion in a rate-pressure environment?

Leibowitz: We hope the rate pressure is ending. The new telecommunications regulation will let the cable companies phase out of the basic and first-tier rates during the next few years. Where they meet any competition, and that would include the provision of wireless cable services by Bell Atlantic and NYNEX, they are immediately deregulated. They also have the opportunity to introduce to the existing tiers new services that are not regulated. For cable modems, they have a fairly broad path downstream, and they are working out the bugs on the upstream (the return path) for simple interactions such as requesting information. The need for a lot of bandwidth is not substantial, but it is needed for video conferencing or massive file transfers. The switching the cable company needs is more for the telephony part of the business and, ultimately, for the switching needed for true video-on-demand rather than near video-on-demand. Cable modems do not need a separate switch.

Question: Can you quantify or give a time frame for any of the new services you mentioned, such as video-on-demand and cable modems?

Leibowitz: The three pieces of equipment we have been waiting for—the cable modem, the telephone interface unit outside the house, and the digital converter—are all due in 1996. The cable modems are beginning to trickle out. The digital converters are supposed to be out by midyear, and the telephone interface units are expected by the end of the year. The cable networks are in the process of upgrading their plant and have another two years to go. The upgrades are about 25 percent or 30 percent done in terms of being telephone ready, but they will not be finished before 1998. The dates of some of the new services depend on regulation, particularly on the telephone side. A number of states have deregulated telephony locally, but until they work out fairer interconnect agreements between the cable operators and the telephone companies, cable is a hit and miss opportunity. The cable legislation has the FCC preempt all state and federal regulations, so we can get some of these new services quicker.

Modem services will be first, because they are virtually here already. Rogers Communications—the largest operator in Canada—is already commercial, and in its first market (about 30,000 homes), it had about 2 percent penetration the first month, which is an encouraging sign, without much promotion. Time Warner, TCI, Continental Cablevision, and Comcast have all announced plans for commercial projects in 1996. Although the digital boxes are expected in mid-1996, I do not see them coming out until late in 1996, which means revenue and profits will begin in 1997. A lot of these services are going to commence in 1998. If the regulations go through, 1998 is when the first meaningful measured business will become apparent on the telephone side. That will be the year when the plant construction will be mostly done. Although the cable modems may come out in 1996, 1998 will be the first year of meaningful impact on the cable industry.

Question: For a telecom player, whether local or long distance, which is a more attractive technology for entry into video delivery—MMDS, LMDS, or DBS?

Leibowitz: MMDS may be the first vehicle readily available. As soon as the digital boxes are ready for cable (mid- to late 1996), they will be ready for MMDS. Bell Atlantic and NYNEX plan to offer MMDS services as soon as they become available. The interesting advantage they have vis-à-vis cable is that once it is ready on a wireless system, it is ready throughout the marketplace. MMDS does not require a slow rebuild of all neighborhoods right away. Bell Atlantic and NYNEX may have an opportunity for a while in some of their markets, but MMDS is probably an interim technology that the RBOCs are using to warehouse customers.

LMDS is wireless cable with more channel capacity than MMDS. It uses an FM digital technology. Cellular Vision has had an experimental system in Brooklyn for a couple of years, but regulations have kept the company from expanding. In many ways, LMDS is a superior technology to MMDS. The problem is logistical. The FCC has to go through the licensing stage, which they are going to do at the rate of two operators in every market, so it will be some time before the licenses are available to offer the system.

DBS is available now on DirecTV. EchoStar launched its first satellite in December and will soon offer 70 or 80 channels. It will have a second satellite up in August 1996, and its service will provide up to 150 channels. Primestar, a DBS operation by a group of cable companies, has a medium-sized dish. MCI and News Corp. jointly bid $700 million on a DBS slot. Either they have to build a satellite, which will take a couple of years, or they will buy satellites from TCI, which has them under construction. MCI and News Corp. will have a service, depending on whether they buy the satellites or not, in the next year or two, so there will be plenty of competition. DBS is an attractive business, but it is a niche business because viewers must spend $600–$800 in equipment and installation, and they do not get local stations. Its appeal is greatest in areas without cable service, although it is getting some share of the cable market. We see DBS as a segment of the market rather than a way to play the whole market.

Question: Do the cable companies have a strong enough brand identity to compete in telephony?

Leibowitz: Recognition is one of the reasons cable companies are teaming up with other companies with brand names. Many companies in the cable industry have a reputation for poor service. They are trying to undo that reputation through customer service efforts, but it is a long-term image problem. By banding together under the Sprint name, TCI, Cox, and Comcast are offering their telephone service to cable companies as Sprint. Also, these services will be offered with discounts, and that incentive may obviate some of the problems of service reputations. Surveys of DirecTV subscribers show that many of them are defectors from standard cable service who were fed up with their cable companies and wanted to get back at the companies for what they perceived as poor service. The surveys also indicate that these subscribers are immensely satisfied with DirecTV's service. The main way the cable companies are getting around their image problem is by changing their names.

Question: Have cable companies lost interest in wired telephony in the United States?

Leibowitz: No. They intend very much to be in wired telephony. Time Warner has a system in Rochester (New York is one of the most liberal states in opening up competition), and it is offering service there, as are AT&T and others. Wired telephony is the biggest potential new market, and the cable companies are eager to serve it. The risk for them is somewhat reduced by the delays in the video entry of the telephone companies. The telephone opportunities—both wireless and wired—are very much at the forefront. Cable modems have received a lot more attention recently because they currently have an advantage no one else has. The boxes are coming, and the consumers love the idea; but that development does not mean that the cable companies are not going to try aggressively to get into the land-line telephone business.

Question: What does the likely eventual launch of PCS imply for cellular revenue growth by the end of the decade? Have we seen a peak in the cellular business?

Leibowitz: In every country that has multiple competitors, the elasticity of demand is such that price competition increases the number of subscribers enough so that the old guys continue to grow along with the new guys. Britain now has two PCS operators and four carriers overall; Sweden has three operators; and we will probably have multiple operators here.

PCS is not a new technology. The British government invented this term for some communications services when it licensed new competition. The theory was that cellular was telephones in cars for business people. They wanted personal communications services representing portable phones for consumers, but the technology is exactly the same, with the only difference being the frequencies used. PCS is essentially cellular, and we believe that the market will expand substantially. American Personal Communications, which is half owned by the Sprint group, was the first to open. It opened in Washington, D.C./Baltimore in mid-November 1995, so December 1995 was its first month of operation. It reportedly signed up 30,000 subscribers in that one month. Interestingly, Bell Atlantic, one of its two competitors, announced that it had a record month in December 1995 for activations, so it is clear that the whole market went up and not entirely at the existing operator's expense. Some of the activity certainly was because a lot of people were fed up with cellular service.

We recently did an offering for a company called Omnipoint Corporation, the first pure PCS stock that has one of the licenses for New York City. In New York City, 40 percent of the cells are busy 50 percent of the time during rush hour—meaning that in 40 percent of the cases people have a 50/50 chance of not getting through or having the call dropped during rush hour. A new digital service that lets you hear crystal clear conversations without being dropped would be a very popular product. Our forecasts in the wireless business are that penetration, which is 12.5 percent now, will pass 20 percent by 1998 and double to more than 40 percent by the end of the next decade. The PCS sector will have about one-third of that market; the old operators, about two-thirds. By that time, they will all be getting equal shares of the still-growing marketplace.

Question: Can the large cable multiple system operators (MSOs) finance the upgrade of their networks for switches without forming ventures with local or long-distance telephone companies?

Leibowitz: They are in the process of upgrading, and they have spent about half of the money they need to spend. To rebuild the cable plant for telephony, they do not have to have financial partners. In some of the newer technologies (such as PCS) that require multibillion dollar investments, they do need partners. Some MSOs already have partners, as is the case with the Sprint consortium and other such partnerships. Some have yet to take on partners. Capital conservation was one of the reasons Time Warner got into a joint venture with U S West. Although the relationship has been acrimonious of late, they are trying to resolve their differences. The big cable capital push is cresting this year and next. After that, the companies will turn cash flow positives. A lot of their incentive to merge now is for strategic alliances as much as for the money.

Question: If content companies are winners because of increased demand for product, why do they want to be vertically integrated?

Leibowitz: Vertical integration gives content companies more control over their own distribution. For instance, New World Communications Group has an alliance with Fox Broadcasting on the programming side. They can distribute their product through the New World stations and the Fox stations. If you are launching a new show and you know you can guarantee it will be carried by more than 40 percent of the country's stations, you have a much better chance of getting it viewed and accepted than if you are a free-standing producer. For example, Liberty Media is a company that is tracking stock of TCI, representing its programming interests. TCI's largest cable operator can offer any programmer distribution to 20 million homes, and that helps the distributor assure himself of an audience and revenues for his products. You capture some of the levels of margin. If Time Warner acquires Turner Broadcasting System, Turner (which owns Castle Rock Entertainment and New Line Cinema) does not need its own movie distribution organization any more; it simply uses the Warner Bros. distribution organization. Turner can drop the entire cost of distribution, so the deal has cost elements that make sense.

Question: If cable modems work as well as it appears they do and cable companies can thereby control access to the Internet, do we get multiple expansion in the stocks?

Leibowitz: I have been trying to push that idea. Cable stocks have not done very well; maybe if the companies add "Internet" to their names, they will get more sponsorship. The companies have the opportunity to provide some of their own services, which may evolve after they provide access to the networks that are already there. If the Internet access or online service access business is growing as rapidly as it is and they have a better mousetrap, they can directly benefit for the next couple of years as they offer that service to all their subscribers. Changing the label does not solve the stock problem, but it helps.

Question: What is your outlook for media/telecom in Eastern Europe? Whom do you see as the beneficiaries?

Leibowitz: It is a country-by-country issue. Most Eastern European countries have very limited government-controlled off-air networks. Eastern Europe has only one public broadcasting company—Central European Media. Other ways do exist, however, for playing international media in the stock market. There are two large international conglomerates that have mostly cable, some DBS, and a little programming. One is United International Holdings, which has a joint venture with Philips Electronics called UPC (United and Philips Communications) in Europe and is the largest European cable operator. TCI International, a company that is 20 percent public and 80 percent owned by U.S.-based TCI, also has some operations in those areas. United International also has interests in Czechoslovakia, but on the broadcast side. Central European Media is the only company I can think of that would be a direct play.

Question: In his presentation, Christopher Dixon theorized that the media world will be dominated by four big players in the future, like the auto industry today. Do you agree? If so, who are they?

Leibowitz: I would not agree with that prediction on a worldwide basis. Companies such as Bertelsmann and Canal Plus are not going to dominate the United States, just as Viacom will not dominate France. The United States will have more than three or four players, although they may come from different angles. On the entertainment side, the dominant ones are News Corp., which owns 20th Century Fox; Viacom; Time Warner; and the Walt Disney Company. You will see some conglomerates on the telephone side. The long-distance carriers will be part of these giant conglomerates. Among the RBOCs, you will see mergers such as Bell Atlantic/NYNEX and perhaps a merger of Pacific Telesis Group with GTE or U S West. These mergers are in the process of formation, so I do not know entirely which companies they will involve, other than the obvious. On the cable side, TCI, Time Warner, Continental Cablevision, Cox, and Comcast are the five dominant players. If they are not part of conglomerates in terms of affiliation and business arrangements, they will be, but they will be different in different areas. Grupo Televisa and Globo are the dominant producers in Latin America, and BSkyB dominates the U.K. market. Three or four companies will not dominate the media industry worldwide.

Question: What single media product or technology do you see as having the greatest impact on consumer households by the year 2005?

Leibowitz: The ability to have entertainment at your fingertips any time day and night and to control that product is an extremely attractive business. Some of it is transfer business. The telephone business is not exciting, but it might be vis-à-vis the cable operators. From the consumers' standpoint, the newest areas would be computer related and transaction related, so the greatest impact would come from the ability to have whatever you want, whenever you want—whether entertainment; transaction services; or interactive shopping, banking, education, and so forth. The highest-impact product will be related to having a dedicated line or lines between the television and computer. The companies that can make that happen will be the biggest beneficiaries.

Distinguishing Characteristics of the Publishing Sector

Peter P. Appert, CFA
Managing Director
Alex. Brown & Sons Inc.

> The growth rate in the publishing sector has lagged behind general GDP growth, but predictions of its death are premature. The free cash flow dynamic of the publishing companies is a meaningful source of their investment appeal. The ability to leverage performance by reinvesting cash flow can be a significant driver of growth and a differentiating factor among the companies. In analyzing the dynamics of this sector, investors should focus on four broad issues: cyclical pressures, technology, competition, and consolidation.

As a print media analyst, I often hear comments from investors that the print medium is dead. Fancy multimedia presentations are the future, and the print medium is going to be buried by the electronic media. I am here to report, however, that the death of print has been grossly exaggerated.

The task of explaining the dynamics of the publishing industry is made more difficult because the publishing business is many different interrelated and sometimes unrelated businesses. At the same time, many of the public media companies are involved in multiple parts of the media business, so analyzing the individual companies requires some understanding of a lot of different businesses.

This presentation begins with a discussion of the dynamics of the publishing sector in terms of size, components, and growth. It then goes into details on the biggest part of the publishing sector, the newspaper sector. From a financial analyst's perspective, newspaper is certainly the most important part of the industry because of its market capitalization, number of public companies, and institutional ownership. Next, the presentation examines the book publishing segment, with particular emphasis on educational publishers because that is also where the market capitalization is largest and, not surprisingly, where investor interest is greatest. The presentation concludes with a discussion of the overriding challenges and opportunities facing the publishing sector. I call these the "four Cs"—cyclical issues, computer issues and the impact of technology on the business, competitive pressures, and consolidation issues.

The Publishing Industry: Overview

Publishing is a big business in the United States, with $83 billion annually coming from the three biggest components of this industry: newspapers ($44 billion), magazines ($21 billion), and books ($18 billion). The aggregate amount is slightly more than 1 percent of GDP.

Publishing is a business that is growing, albeit at a modest pace. The cumulative average annual growth rate (CAGR) over a recent five-year period reflects the sad reality that all three of these components of the publishing business have had growth rates lower than GDP growth. From 1989 to 1994, newspapers, magazines, and books had a CAGR of 3.7 percent, 3.5 percent, and 5.2 percent, respectively, compared with 5.3 percent for GDP. Those figures probably understate the growth rate of these industries to some extent because of the cyclical nature of the industry and a nasty advertising recession in the early 1990s—the worst in the postwar period.

Publishing is clearly a changing business. The sources of change are multifaceted. Short-term cyclical issues drive the business. Technology creates tremendous opportunity and also tremendous challenges for publishers. The competition for advertisers' dollars and for readers' time is a significant issue. Also, the publishing business is undergoing significant consolidation. These forces of change are reviewed later in this presentation.

In this business, many of the big media companies have their toes in a lot of ponds. For example, Capital Cities/ABC, best known as a broadcaster and now as part of Disney, is one of the largest newspaper publishers in the United States. News Corp., best known in the United States for its movie and broadcasting operations, is also one of the largest book publishers.

Newspapers

The newspaper subsector accounts for roughly half of the total revenue of the publishing industry. There are a dozen-plus large public newspaper companies, including Gannett, Knight-Ridder, New York Times, Tribune, and Times Mirror.

This section addresses the basics of the newspaper sector from an operating standpoint, current operating trends, stock valuation and performance, and the long-term issues facing the industry.

Operating Basics

The revenue dynamics of the newspaper business from a fundamental operating standpoint are easy to understand. There are two key drivers of revenue in this business—advertising, which contributes about 80 percent of newspaper revenue, and circulation, which contributes about 20 percent. This 80/20 split between advertising and circulation has been fairly consistent over the years. Typically, newspaper publishers become more aggressive with circulation pricing in years when the ad market is weak cyclically, but the pricing flexibilities are limited in this business.

Total newspaper advertising revenues of about $34.2 billion in 1994 can be broken down into three main categories: retail, classified, and national. **Figure 1** provides the details. The retail category accounts for roughly half of all advertising revenues, classified advertising contributes more than a third of revenues, and national advertising provides a little more than a tenth.

Retail advertising is not only the largest portion of advertising revenue but also the most troubling. The consolidation among retailers, the increasing competition for retail advertising dollars, and the shift in retailers' ad budgets away from print and into electronic media has resulted in very modest growth rates in retail ad revenues for newspapers in recent years. At the same time, newspaper publishers have found raising retail ad rates increasingly difficult and instead have become more

Figure 1. Newspaper Industry Revenue Dynamics

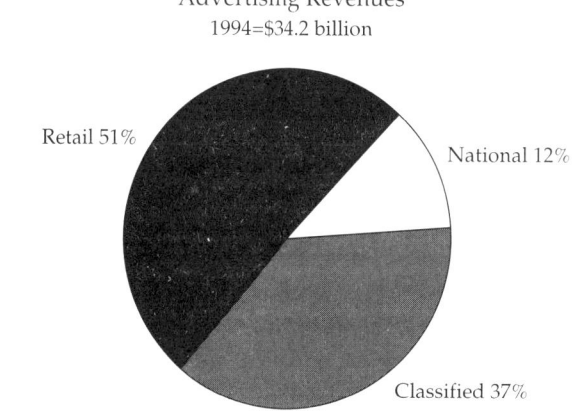

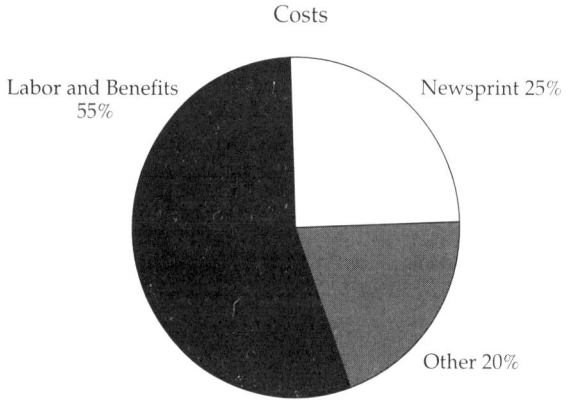

Source: Peter P. Appert, based on data from Newspaper Association of America (NAA), U.S. Department of Commerce, and Alex. Brown & Sons estimates.

aggressive in raising classified ad rates.

Classified advertising is by far the most profitable component of newspaper ad revenues. Because the revenues per inch of space in the newspaper are significantly higher in the classified sector than they are in the retail sector, the profitability of classified is higher. However, because classified consists primarily of help-wanted or employment ads (which account for about half of the total in the classified sector), automotive advertising, and real estate ads, it is highly correlated to economic activity and interest rates. As a result, it also tends to be extremely cyclical. So, when the economy is strong, newspaper publishers do extremely well because classified revenue tends to rise rapidly. When the economy is weak, newspaper publishers pay the price in terms of declining classified advertising.

Newspaper publishers have done relatively poorly in the national advertising market. They have given up a significant share of national advertising dollars during the past couple of decades to other more nationally visible media, such as television. The largest national ad categories are travel, much of which is related to airline price wars, and advertisements from the financial services sector.

The cost side of the newspaper equation is also easy to understand. Newspaper costs have two main drivers: paper and people, as shown in the lower panel of Figure 1. Total labor and benefits account for a little more than half of total operating expenses, and newsprint represents somewhere in the neighborhood of one-fourth of expenses. The "other" category includes everything else: ink, electricity, depreciation—the usual items. Figure 1 demonstrates that this is still a labor-intensive business.

The physical production and delivery of a daily newspaper is a complex manufacturing undertaking. The publisher has a short window in which to print an edition and deliver it, with no room for mistakes. If the newspaper misses today's production, it cannot make it up tomorrow. The product is gone, along with those ad dollars. This situation contributes to the labor intensity of the industry.

Current Operating Trends

The current trends in this industry create a good-news/bad-news scenario. The good news is that labor costs are stable. **Figure 2** shows a secular shift downward in wage inflation. Some might say the entire U.S. economy has experienced a secular shift downward in wage inflation, but if newspaper wages are compared with overall wage inflation in the U.S. economy, the difference is apparent. In the 1970s, newspaper wage inflation exceeded the U.S. average, but it has been significantly below the U.S. average in the 1980s and early 1990s. Productivity in this industry (output per worker-hour) has also improved significantly, largely because advanced production facilities, computerized page layout, and other technology-driven improvements have reduced the industry's staffing requirements.

In effect, during the past decade, newspaper publishers have traded labor for capital. In some ways, the situation is analogous to that of the railroad industry. Productivity gains driven by technology have resulted in a large improvement in operating margins and in profitability in the railroad industry. Newspaper publishers have the potential for an equally dramatic improvement in margins driven by productivity. In the short run, however, margins are being constrained by sharply higher paper costs. Just when the newspaper publishers had succeeded in reducing labor costs and just when the ad business was beginning to recover in 1994, newspaper publishers suffered the most dramatic and painful increases in paper prices in the postwar period.

In the past 12 months, the cost per ton of newsprint has risen about 40 percent. In fact, in 1995, six

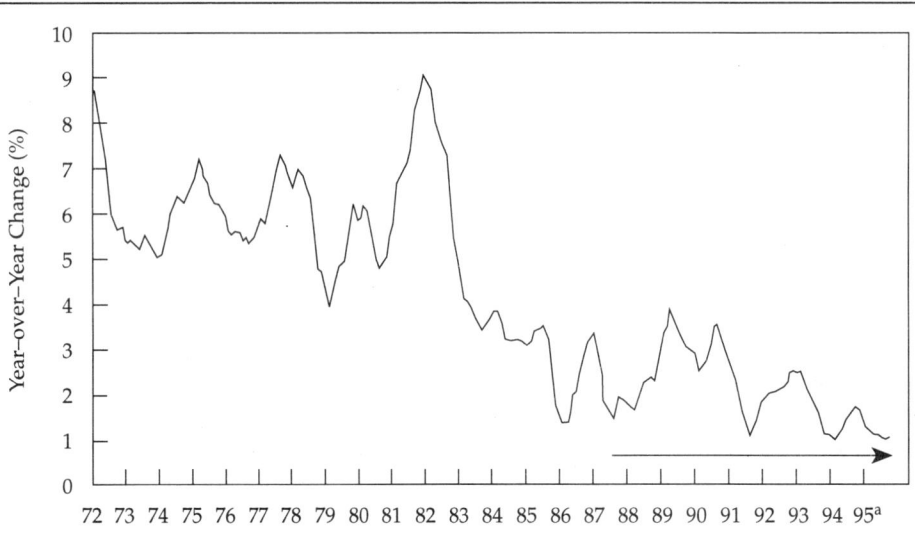

Figure 2. Labor Costs, 1972–95
(average hourly earnings)

Note: Data based on six-month moving average.

[a]1995 data are through September.

Source: Peter P. Appert, based on data from DRI/McGraw-Hill and Alex. Brown estimates.

Figure 3. Newsprint Costs, 1980–96
(East Coast delivery)

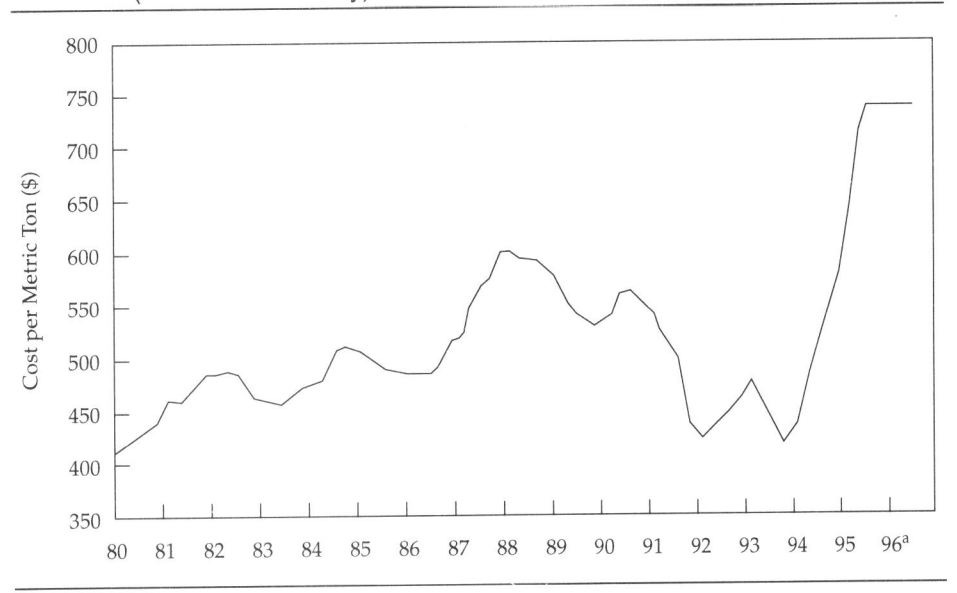

ᵃ1996 data based on estimates.

Source: Peter P. Appert, based on data from industry sources.

years' worth of newsprint price increases were condensed into one year. The good news is that newsprint prices appear to be stabilizing now, as shown in **Figure 3**. In my opinion, paper prices will start declining by the end of 1996. The paper manufacturers got a bit ahead of themselves in the magnitude and speed of the paper price increases during 1995, but new capacity overseas combined with reduced domestic consumption is shifting the balance of pricing power within the newsprint industry. Because of the commodity nature of the newsprint business and the magnitude of the price increase, the conclusion that newsprint prices are stabilizing is probably a safe and supportable one. The good news for publishers is that most newsprint manufacturers have already pushed back a scheduled February 1 price increase to March 1 and now to April 1.

The bad news is that revenue growth is clearly slowing, as shown in **Figure 4**. The advertising revenue chart is a monthly index for the 12 largest public newspaper companies, and it provides a good snapshot of what is happening in the industry. The growth in advertising revenue peaked in late 1994 and has been decelerating since. Decelerating revenue growth has significant negative implications for industry margins and profitability and, therefore, stock performance.

The same trend is apparent in the help-wanted advertising index, shown in **Figure 5**. Because the classified category and the help-wanted subcategory are the most cyclical components of industry revenues, they serve as good coincident indicators of economic activity. The index merely reflects what we already know, that the economy is slowing. Because classified is the most profitable category and help wanted is the most profitable

Figure 4. Newspaper Industry Advertising Revenue, 1988–95

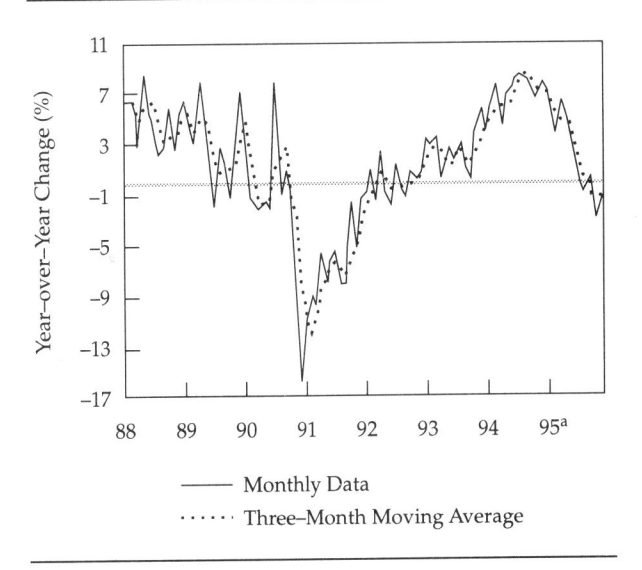

— Monthly Data
····· Three–Month Moving Average

ᵃ1995 data are through November.

Source: Peter P. Appert, based on data from company reports and Alex. Brown estimates.

The Media Industry

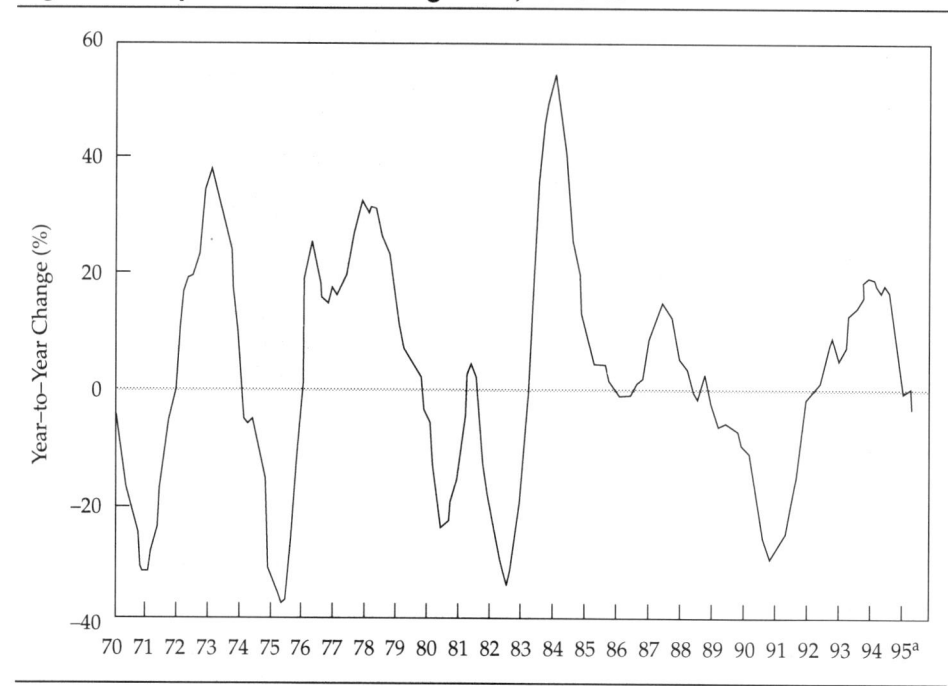

Figure 5. Help-Wanted Advertising Index, 1970–95

[a]1995 data are through November.
Source: Peter P. Appert, based on data from the Conference Board.

subcomponent of classified, the decline in help-wanted volume is bad news for the industry's short-term profitability.

Countervailing forces are at work. On the positive side, newspaper currently has no labor inflation and is getting productivity benefits from that side of the equation. Paper costs appear to be stabilizing and may even decline. The problem is that the revenue dynamics will make the difference in short-term earnings and earnings per share. In the context of decelerating ad revenue growth, the newspaper stocks are likely to underperform the market.

Valuation

The newspaper stocks have not been stellar performers in recent years. The top panel of **Figure 6** shows that newspaper stocks recently returned to their 1987 highs, but analysts are more interested in the returns relative to the market, as shown in the lower panel of Figure 6. The monthly data tell an interesting story: During the past couple of decades, investors have needed to make only two long-term decisions regarding the newspaper group. In the 1970s and 1980s, they wanted to own these stocks. The dynamic of a higher inflation rate, impressive secular revenue growth, and manageable cost dynamics produced strong earnings gains and made these stocks the darlings of Wall Street. In the 1990s, the stocks have underperformed the market substantially as a result of the combination of recent paper price increases and long-term issues of relatively modest ad revenue growth.

Investors have two ways of thinking about these stocks from a valuation standpoint. The first approach, illustrated in the top panel of **Figure 7**, is straightforward and traditional. Here the focus is on standard P/E analysis, in which the stocks trade on a P/E multiple basis relative to the market. In the second approach, shown in the lower panel of Figure 7, the focus is on the cash flow dynamics of the business. In this case, total enterprise value or equity market capitalization plus debt minus cash divided by earnings before interest, taxes, depreciation, and amortization (EBITDA) is one of the standards by which investors evaluate this group. It is also the standard on which acquisition analysis is based.

Figure 7 shows that, despite the underperformance of the group, the stocks are actually trading at close to their average historical valuation levels, indicating that the earnings dynamic has not been all that impressive recently. So, the stocks have underperformed, but the earnings have underperformed just as much. As a result, the stocks look fairly to fully valued.

Long-Term Issues

Several long-term issues will make the difference in whether these stocks continue to underperform or

Figure 6. Newspaper Industry Performance, 1970–95

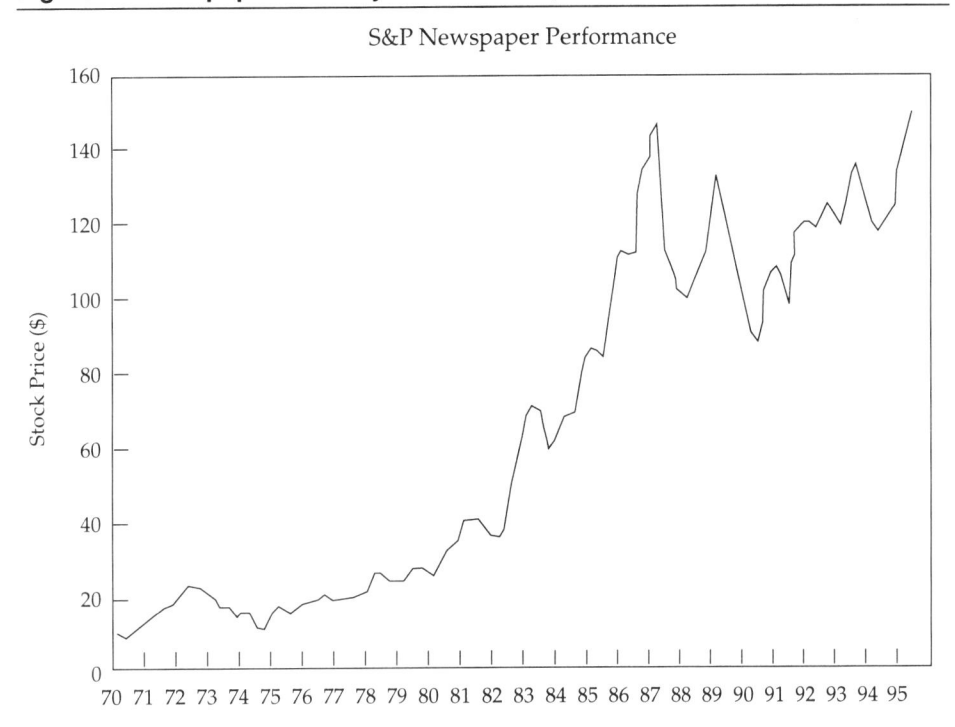

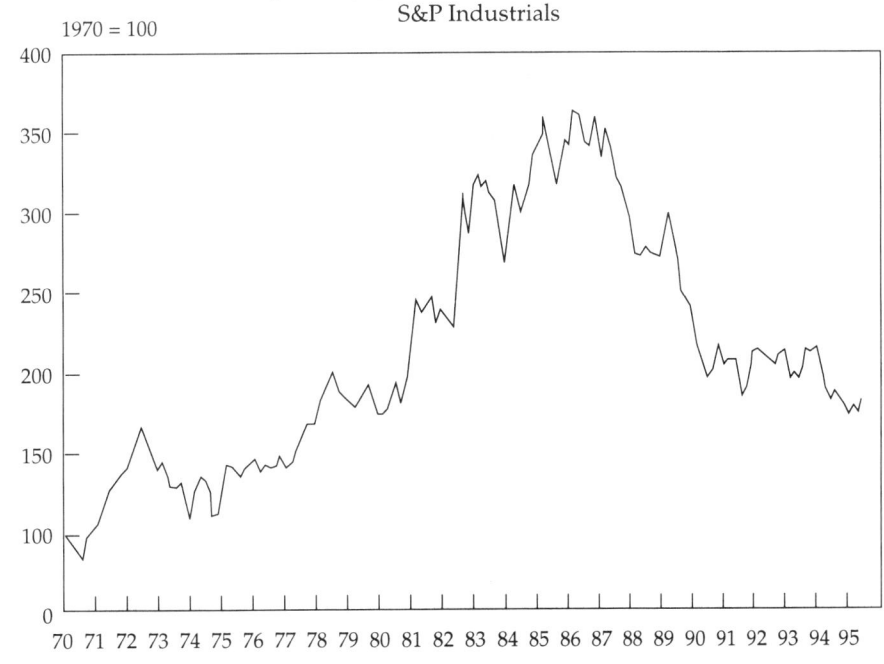

S&P Newspaper Performance

Monthly Newspaper Price Performance Relative to the S&P Industrials

1970 = 100

Source: Peter P. Appert, based on data from Standard & Poor's Corporation and Alex. Brown estimates.

Figure 7. Valuation Criteria

S&P Newspaper Index Trailing P/E Relative to the S&P Industrials, 1974–96

Newspaper Industry Total Market Value to EBITDA, October 1986 to January 1996

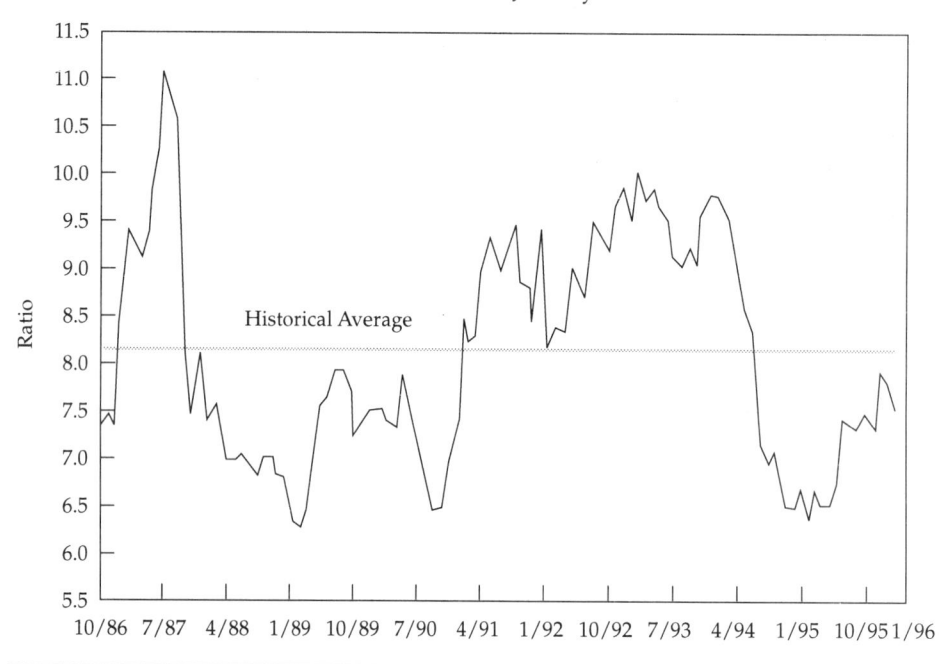

Note: Data for both panels are through January 1996.

Source: Peter P. Appert, based on data from company reports, Standard & Poor's, and Alex. Brown estimates.

Figure 8. Newspaper Industry Circulation, 1960–94

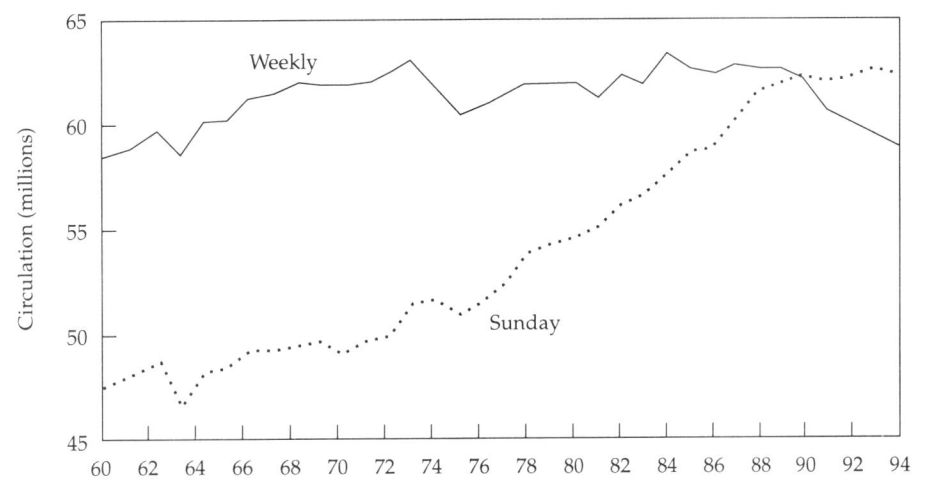

Source: Peter P. Appert, based on data from *Editor & Publisher* and Alex. Brown estimates.

whether money can be made in them. The big issues are trends in circulation, which is a measure of the underlying health of this subsector; the cyclical issues already discussed; competition; and technology changes.

The circulation side of the equation, as shown in **Figure 8**, is an interesting issue. The line on top is daily circulation, which has been essentially flat for the past 30 years or so. The rising line is the Sunday circulation, which has been the success story. Sunday circulation has risen pretty consistently, although it also has actually been relatively flat for the past couple of years. The Sunday paper can account for as much as 50 percent of a daily newspaper's revenues and earnings, so the long-term growth in circulation on Sundays has been a meaningful positive. Competition from other media is less intense on Sunday. People are still in the habit of spending some time reading a newspaper on Sundays, whereas on weekdays, they are more harried and have less time for the newspaper.

In true analytical fashion, Figure 8 presents the data in the way that looks most favorable. **Figure 9**, on the other hand, presents the data in perhaps a more honest way—household penetration of newspapers in the United States. The newspaper industry has done a poor job of selling the newspaper habit to readers. This decline in household penetration is a bit misleading, however, in the sense that

Figure 9. Newspaper Household Penetration, 1960–94

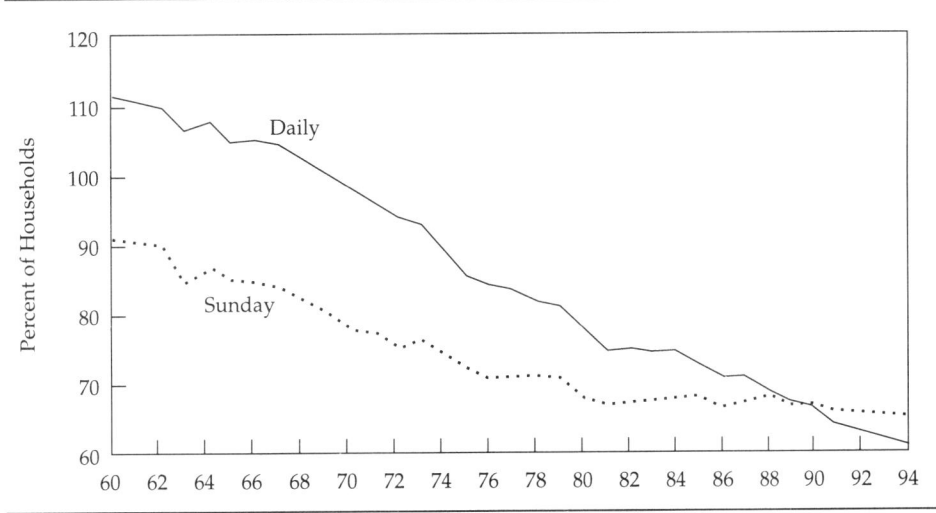

Source: Peter P. Appert, based on data from *Editor & Publisher* and Alex. Brown estimates.

The Media Industry   35

in the past 30 years, U.S. newspapers have gone from a competitive business with multiple newspapers in every city to one that is essentially monopolistic. Approximately 1,400 daily newspapers currently are published in the United States, but only 12 markets have two competing, separately owned newspapers. That situation means a lot of newspapers consolidated or went out of business in the past several decades, a trend that translates into declining household penetration. At the same time, the effect of fewer competitive newspaper markets has translated into substantially improved cash flow margins for the survivors. When competitors go out of business, there is an opportunity to pick up incremental circulation and incremental ad dollars, and the pricing pressures ease. That secular trend has helped this business during the past decade, but that process is largely finished at this point.

The competitive issue is key. The newspaper publishers face competition not only for advertisers' dollars but also for the readers' time. The competitors for advertisers' dollars are numerous and include—among others—television, cable, and direct mail. The newspaper industry, because it has the biggest slice of the advertising pie at this point, is the obvious target for new media coming into the marketplace. As for the issue of readers' time, consider the implications for daily and Sunday circulation of increased competition from new media. To the extent that people spend time surfing the Internet and playing video games, they have less time for newspapers. Such a trend has significant implications for publishers and for all traditional media.

Although our discussion thus far has had a cautionary tone, the newspaper industry has several very positive aspects. Perhaps the most significant aspect is the cash-generating capacity of a well-run newspaper. The free cash flow dynamics of the newspaper publishing business are, in general, wonderful. Capital spending tends to be lumpy. A publisher must build a plant to physically produce a paper, but once built, it may not require meaningful upgrades for 30 years or more. As a result, free cash flow (cash flow minus capital spending and dividends) tends to be positive.

At the same time—and this point is very relevant in an era of rapid technological change—the newspaper publishers, particularly the quality newspaper publishers, have brand names and content that can be leveraged in an environment in which new distribution channels are developing rapidly. Electronic delivery of the traditional newspaper is an emerging market on which a lot of money is being spent currently but not a lot of money is being made yet. Nevertheless, these online services potentially represent significant revenue flow and a new way for newspapers to grow.

Although a lot of money is being spent on experiments and not a lot of money is being made, some examples provide an indication of the direction in which the industry is moving. The *New York Times* for many years has sold its content through the LEXIS-NEXIS online information services. That contract has recently been renegotiated. The estimated fee income to the *Times* from selling its content electronically is in excess of $20 million a year—a significant revenue source. Clearly, the concept of taking existing content and selling it again can be extremely profitable.

The *San Jose Mercury News*, which is a Knight-Ridder paper, has one of the best Web sites and is starting to generate some meaningful revenue by selling—via the Internet—classified advertising and access to content material that is not in the print paper. The newspapers collect much more information through their reporters each day than they can physically fit into the paper. Some folks are willing to pay a premium to go beyond what is in the paper and get greater details from an electronic medium.

I estimate that more than half of the newspapers in the United States currently have some form of electronic product, something that is accessible right now, and I would expect that within the next couple of years, virtually all of them will have some electronic products in the marketplace. This development might be significant to the valuation of the newspaper stocks.

Book Publishers

Book publishing, which makes up about a quarter of the total revenue of the publishing industry, is composed of two separate sectors: the educational/professional publishers and the trade publishers, which are the general-interest publishers. Among the best-known public book publishers are Harcourt General, Houghton Mifflin Company, Scholastic, and McGraw-Hill Companies. The magazine business also accounts for roughly a quarter of publishing industry revenues. Not a lot of pure magazine publishers are left in the United States. Meredith Publishing is probably the best example. Other major players in the magazine business are Time Warner, which is the largest magazine publisher in the world (although the magazine business now represents a relatively small piece of its total business), and Reader's Digest Association.

The following sections focus on the operating fundamentals of book publishers and what drives their growth; the stocks, how they have done, and how investors think about them from a valuation standpoint; the current outlook and trends in the business; and the long-term issues affecting book publishers.

Operating Fundamentals

The operating components of the U.S. book publishing business are shown in **Figure 10**. Book publishing is best considered as two separate businesses: the educational/professional publishing business and the general or trade publishing business. These sectors are quite different in their consumers and their economics.

Educational/professional publishers can be characterized by four observations. First, their operating margins tend to be high—for educational publishers, margins are consistently in the mid- to high teens; and among professional publishers (legal, medical, scientific), the industry standard is 20–25 percent. Second, this business has very significant barriers to entry. A successful start-up is rarely seen in this business because of the heavy capital costs required to create the product and the difficulty of establishing a brand name. Third, the revenue dynamic tends to be very predictable. Fourth, the potential leverage to growth provided by technology is particularly relevant because the content produced by the educational and professional publisher frequently can be repackaged for delivery electronically or through alternative distribution channels.

Trade and general publishing companies have much lower margins than educational/professional publishers, and the barriers to entry in trade and general publishing are also quite low. Small players come and go regularly, and predicting which publisher is going to be hot is quite difficult. To some extent, trade/general publishing is like the movie business in that it can be hit driven and, therefore, unpredictable. The niche publishers—the ones that have some particular focus or expertise, whether it is their distribution channel (e.g., direct-mail marketing) or a particular market niche (e.g., children's publishing, cookbooks, travel)—do best. In general, however, the trade publishing business has not been all that profitable in recent years because of unpredictable revenue streams, rising author advances, excessive product returns from retailers, and pressure on margins from book retailers.

My focus is on the educational and professional publishing side of the business because it seems to be the more important and appealing segment economically. The educational publishing business can be segmented as shown in **Figure 11**. The college segment accounts for about half the business, and the elementary and high school segment—or

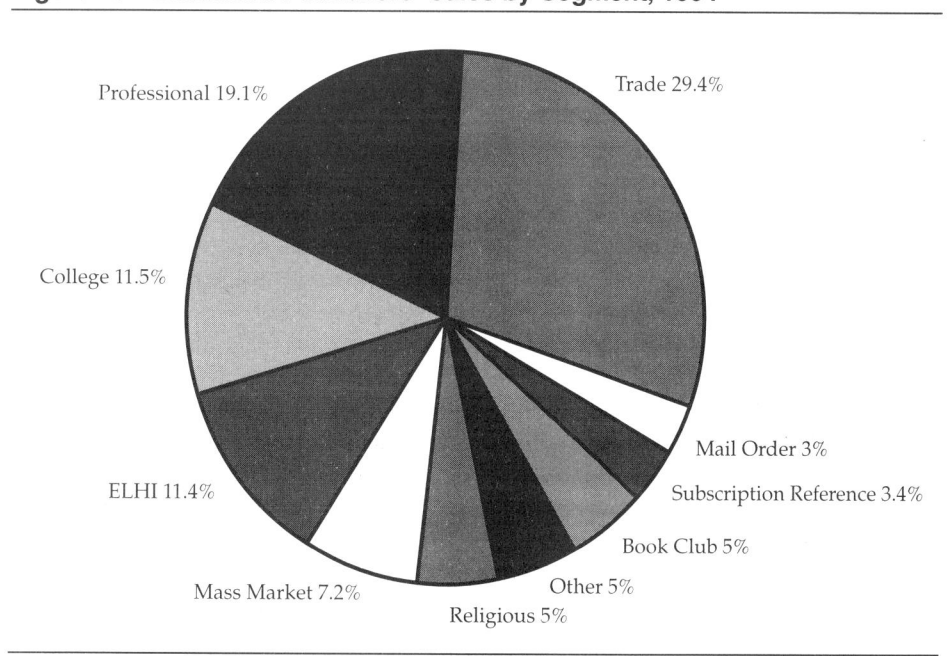

Figure 10. Estimated Publishers' Sales by Segment, 1994

- Professional 19.1%
- Trade 29.4%
- College 11.5%
- ELHI 11.4%
- Mass Market 7.2%
- Religious 5%
- Other 5%
- Book Club 5%
- Subscription Reference 3.4%
- Mail Order 3%

Note: "Other" category includes university presses, standardized tests, and miscellaneous items.
Source: Peter P. Appert, based on data from the Association of American Publishers.

Figure 11. Educational Publishing Market: Estimated Sales by Segment, 1994

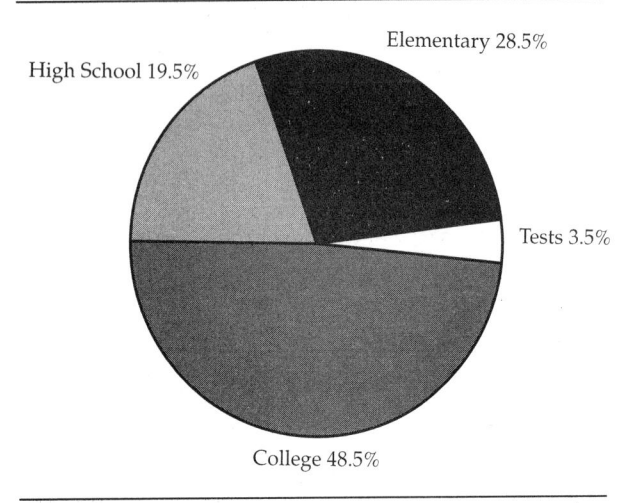

- Elementary 28.5%
- High School 19.5%
- Tests 3.5%
- College 48.5%

Source: Peter P. Appert, based on data from the Association of American Publishers and Alex. Brown estimates.

"ELHI"—is roughly the other half; together they represent about $4.5 billion in revenues.

Three forces drive the educational publishing business and make it intriguing from an analytical standpoint. The first driver—demographics—is shown in **Figure 12**. The population of school-age children is growing in the United States. This "echo baby boom" is the most important driver of unit demand in the educational publishing business.

One appealing aspect of this industry—from an analytical point of view—is that some mystery is taken out of the business by the predictability of the demographic cycle. As an example, note that the number of kindergartners in four years is already known because the children have already been born. **Figure 13** shows that the enrollment of ELHI students in the United States bottomed in 1984 and, in 1996, will surpass the previous peak in total enrollments that was reached in 1971. Beyond that, the population of school-age kids will continue to grow at a pretty impressive rate for another several years, after which the rate of growth slows. We will not reach the peak in this current enrollment cycle until well beyond 2005. Not many businesses allow a high-confidence 10-year guarantee, at least in terms of the unit demand characteristics.

The second driver of growth beyond unit demand or enrollment growth is the textbook adoption cycle. A unique wrinkle within the educational publishing business is that roughly half the states choose to buy their textbooks at the state level, a process called textbook adoption. The state board of education typically determines which book should be replaced in a given year and screens publishers'

Figure 12. Annual Number of Live Births in the United States, 1946–94

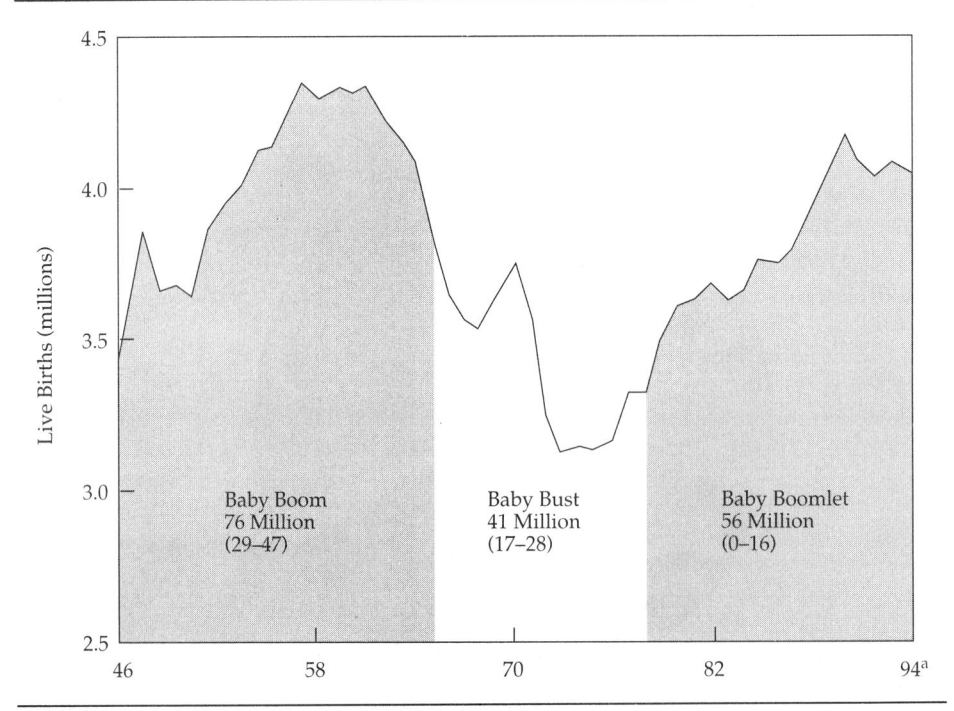

- Baby Boom: 76 Million (29–47)
- Baby Bust: 41 Million (17–28)
- Baby Boomlet: 56 Million (0–16)

[a]1994 data are projected.

Source: Peter P. Appert, based on data from U.S. Department of Education.

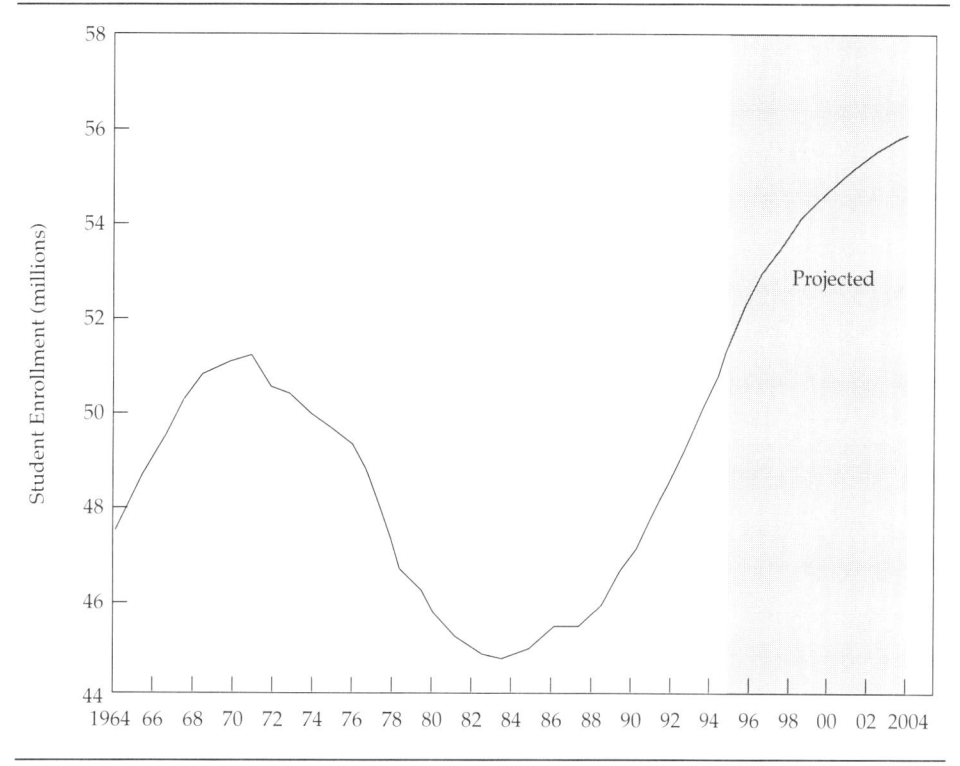

Figure 13. Total Student Enrollment (K–12)

Source: Peter P. Appert, based on data from the U.S. Department of Education and Alex. Brown estimates.

offerings to decide what to approve. Those publishers are then permitted to sell within that state.

The reason this process is significant is because it provides an additional level of visibility to publishers' revenues. If I know that Florida is buying reading textbooks in 1996 and that Florida is a relatively large state in total student enrollments, that knowledge helps me build from the bottom up a good model of industry revenues. When a convergence of several adoptions occurs in important disciplines in important states in a given year, publishers obviously will have significant revenue growth in that year. The megayear of this decade in terms of state textbook adoptions will probably be 1997, when three of the largest states—California, Texas, and Florida, which together have about 25 percent of total student enrollments—plan adoptions in three major disciplines: reading, math, and science.

Figure 14 indicates which are the adoption states and which are the open states. Most of the adoption states are in the South and West. Open territories (primarily the northern states) let the local school districts decide when and where to spend their textbook money.

The funding environment is the third and perhaps the most controversial of the major issues driving the educational publishers. Although not a broadly accepted view, some observers (myself included) believe the funding environment in U.S. schools has improved in recent years. The real issue is state and local tax receipts: About 94 percent of school funding comes from state and local government; only about 6 percent comes from the federal government. The good news is that federal spending on education has gone up slightly in recent years. More importantly, improving tax receipts at the state and local level, which primarily reflect improved economic activity, have taken off some of the pressure from a funding standpoint.

For investors, the three observations above translate into favorable industry trends driven by rising unit demand because of the secular growth in enrollments, leveraged by a favorable trend in textbook adoption schedules. If these variables are combined with a funding environment that at minimum has stabilized and may be improving, the net result is an acceleration in revenue growth. Given the significant scale economies in this industry, as revenue growth improves, margins rise. Not surprisingly, therefore, these stocks have done considerably better than those of the newspaper industry in recent years.

Stock Performance and Valuation

Stocks of educational publishers have basically performed well, as **Figure 15** confirms. This figure

Figure 14. Adoption versus Open-Territory States

☐ Adoption States: School districts purchase educational materials that have been "adopted" at the state level in order to qualify for state funding.

▨ Open Territory States: School districts purchase educational materials independently.

▪ Georgia and Oregon: Issue state-recommended lists but do not tie purchasing to funding.

Source: Alex. Brown & Sons.

is significantly distorted by the inclusion of Houghton Mifflin, which has been a substantial laggard among all the publishers. Without Houghton, the educational publishing sector has significantly outperformed the market.

The market values educational publishers' stocks much as it values other publishers, including the newspaper companies. Typically, analysts look at both the traditional earnings multiple and cash flow multiples. On average, the educational publishers sell at multiples of 7–8 times operating cash flow. In that sense, from the valuation standpoint, the market does not differentiate significantly between the newspaper companies and the educational publishers. That valuation anomaly creates opportunity: In our view, the educational publishers are cheap relative to the newspapers by a significant margin. Given the superior fundamentals of the business and the superior potential for revenue and earnings growth, we believe these companies could experience an upward revaluation in their multiples over the next couple of years.

In terms of the recent numbers, the growth rate of the educational publishing business is superior to that of the newspaper business. Top-line growth in educational publishing should be in the neighborhood of 8 percent for the print side and significantly higher for the electronic side, with educational software growing in excess of 20 percent a year, as shown in **Table 1**. The traditional educational publishers are becoming major players in the software business, which should have a positive impact on their growth rates.

Long-Term Trends

In the long term, technology creates significant opportunities for the educational publishers, as it does for all print media businesses. Potentially, it is

Figure 15. Index of Educational Publishers' Stock Performance

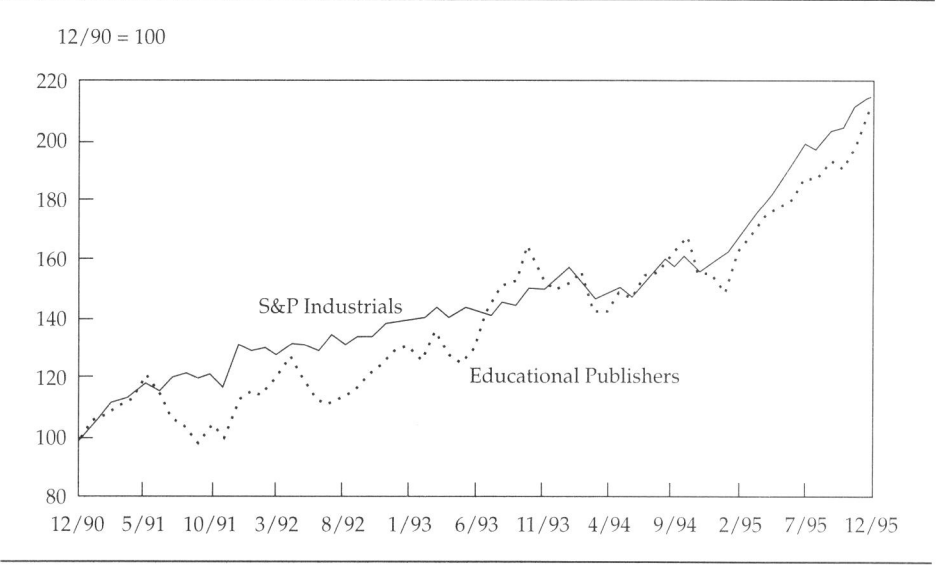

Note: Dates shown are for last day of month.

Source: Alex. Brown & Sons, based on data from Standard & Poor's.

also a significant threat. The opportunity for the educational publishers, however, is dramatic in terms of the leverageability of their proprietary content. In many ways, the educational publishing business could be thought of as similar to the movie business in the early 1980s. The movie companies concluded that their traditional business—the creation of theatrical films for distribution through theater circuits—was maturing. They discovered that if they took their proprietary content, the theatrical film, and packaged it differently—into a video, for example—they could sell the same product twice. In fact, the revenue dynamics of the movie business have changed in that the home video market is significantly larger than the theatrical distribution channel.

That change is potentially very analogous to the process that is occurring right now in the educational publishing business. The educational publishers own proprietary content (their print-based curriculum material) that can be enhanced and repackaged for distribution in a multimedia format. This multimedia product can then be sold not only to the traditional school market but, more importantly, directly to the

Table 1. Instructional Media Spending

Product	1994 $millions	1994 Percentage of Total	1998 (estimated) $millions	1998 (estimated) Percentage of Total	Estimated Growth Rate
Print material					
ELHI textbooks	$2,300.0	40%	$3,130.0	38%	8%
College textbooks	2,100.0	36	2,750.0	33	7
Tests	300.0	5	440.0	5	10
Total	$4,700.0	81%	$6,320.0	77%	8%
Electronic materials					
Software (including CD-ROMs)	$400.0	7%	$925.0	11%	23%
Videos, broadcast/satellite services, online services, etc.	370.0	6	572.0	7	12
Instructional learning systems	310.0	5	420.0	5	8
Total	$1,080.0	19%	$1,917.0	23%	15%
Total spending	$5,780.0	100%	$8,237.0	100%	9%

Note: Numbers may not add to totals because of rounding.

Source: Peter P. Appert, based on data from the Association of American Publishers, Book Industry Study Group, SIMBA International, and Alex. Brown estimates.

The Media Industry

consumer market. For example, the parent whose child uses the Harcourt math program in class will have an opportunity to buy a supplemental product for home use that builds on the material the child is already using each day in school. For Harcourt, this represents incremental revenue with potentially very attractive margins.

As a measure of the potential significance of the multimedia market to educational publishers, consider the following example. In the United States, schools currently spend about $43 per child each year on all forms of instructional material. That includes textbooks, workbooks, tests. If I choose to buy *Wiggleworks* (the CD-ROM supplement to Scholastic's reading program) for my child to use at home, I will pay in the neighborhood of $43 for it. Effectively, I am doubling per capita spending on instructional material in my home by buying this product.

The implication for the educational publishers is extraordinary because the potential profit margins of these new products are substantially higher than their existing products. Having already spent $50 million or more to create a new print-based reading program, the incremental investment required for a multimedia version of this product is relatively modest. Therefore, as publishers distribute their product through this new channel, they should enjoy an acceleration in revenue growth accompanied by an expansion in margins. All of the traditional educational publishers—Harcourt, McGraw-Hill, Houghton Mifflin, for example—are working to expand their multimedia product lines and these companies should be the major players.

The other long-term issue to note in the educational publishing business is the continuing process of consolidation. About 10–15 years ago, the educational publishing business consisted of a dozen or so major players. Depending on how the business is segmented, only four to six major players remain. This reduction has occurred because of the significant scale economies in educational publishing, which have encouraged market share growth via acquistion. These companies, like the newspaper publishers, also tend to generate free cash flow, so they have been able to accelerate growth via acquisition. Just over the course of the past few months, Houghton Mifflin acquired D.C. Heath & Company and News Corp. sold Scott Foresman Publishing Company to a British publisher, Pearson (parent company of Addison-Wesley). Both of these transactions further concentrated revenues in this business and should contribute to improved margins in educational publishing.

Conclusion

In analyzing the dynamics of the publishing industry, investors should focus on four broad issues: cyclical pressures, technology, competition, and consolidation. These factors are likely to be the key drivers of industry stock performance for the foreseeable future.

Although predicting the ups and downs of the economic cycle is obviously challenging, investors should attempt to own the newspaper stocks early in the economic cycle, at the first indications that ad revenue growth might be improving. That point is when newspaper publishers have the greatest leverage in revenue growth and earnings.

The positive implications of technological change are dramatic, but for the newspaper publishers, that opportunity contains a threat as well. If publishers allow competitors to get ahead of them in the electronic delivery of classified advertising, that important reserve source could be at risk. At the same time, newspaper publishers own significant proprietary content and have brands that can be leveraged through electronic distribution channels. For book publishers, technology has potentially large, positive implications for long-term industry growth and profitability through the creation of new products and new distribution channels.

The advertising marketplace is characterized by a high level of competition. Successful newspaper publishers must constantly seek to grow circulation, improve their editorial product, and create new products to maintain or improve their share of the local advertising market. The educational publishing business has a limited number of large players, but competition for market share is intense. The consolidation process that is ongoing in educational publishing should serve to ease these pressures somewhat.

The free cash flow dynamics of the publishing companies are a meaningful source of their investment appeal. The ability to leverage performance by reinvesting cash flow can be a significant driver of growth and a significant differentiating factor among the companies. The companies that have consistently done the best job in reinvesting their free cash flow—whether through acquistions, share repurchases, or other uses—have been the better performers from an investment perspective. Not surprisingly, the companies that have been less successful in reinvesting their cash flow (or the companies in which the managements have been shareholder unfriendly in using their cash flow) have been much weaker performers secularly from a stock standpoint.

Question and Answer Session

Peter P. Appert, CFA

Question: How can we find out and stay current on which states are planning adoptions, how much they plan to buy on which topics, and which publishers have been selected?

Appert: Keeping up on these matters is challenging. The reality is that there is no one source from which you can keep current on this information easily and conveniently. No trade publication summarizes it. I regularly call publishing contacts to try to get a sense of what is happening. I call state and local boards of education as the adoption process is going on, trying to get a sense of what the districts are thinking. The process is very labor intensive.

Who is adopting what discipline is public information. Companies will provide input on this. Determining who is winning in the adoption process is where your analytical stealth comes in handy, because you need to go out and do some real field work. Short of working full time on this project, you are probably going to have to rely on someone like me, whose focus is this sector, to help you out.

Question: What is the risk that states might come together to form buying groups? These groups could then demand discounts, thus cutting margins.

Appert: The states choose to retain a certain level of "personalization" of textbooks for local requirements. You might think that a math book would work in California the same way it works in New York. In fact, California has its own thoughts on the appropriate math curriculum and, therefore, the format of its math textbooks. To some extent, the state's desire to exert control over curriculum and textbooks precludes the types of buying groups suggested in the question.

Pricing in the educational publishing business is an interesting issue because—and maybe this is a function of selling to the public sector—pricing is generally not a competitive issue. The price points of the educational publishers do not differ significantly. A basic math book used at the elementary or high school level might cost about $25. In addition, sales of supplementals (workbooks, tests, and other such items) can push this dollar amount higher. Textbook purchases represent less than 1 percent of a school's budget. Because this number is so small, it makes pricing less of a focus.

Question: You mention that there are four to six educational publishers. Who are they?

Appert: The big four or six, depending on how we want to count them, would be as follows, from largest to smallest: (1) Simon & Schuster (a division of Viacom), which includes Prentice Hall; (2) Macmillan/McGraw-Hill, a division of McGraw-Hill Companies; (3) Harcourt Brace & Company, a division of Harcourt General; (4) Houghton Mifflin; and (5) Scott Foresman, which was recently sold by News Corp. to Pearson. Scholastic is an emerging player in the market.

Question: Can you share with us which of these companies or others you think are well positioned for the long term?

Appert: Scholastic has done an unusually good job in positioning itself for the secular issues driving this business. Scholastic's main business is selling children's books into the consumer and school market through book clubs and book fairs. Parents with young kids might be familiar with the circular that their children bring home from school every month, offering a selection of low-cost, high-quality children's books. The average price of the high-quality paperback book you are buying through the Scholastic book club is not much higher than $2. That business has been exceptionally attractive for the same demographic reasons that the educational publishing business is attractive.

What differentiates Scholastic is that it has taken its brand name and its proprietary content—products such as its book series *The Magic School Bus*, *Goosebumps*, and *The Baby-Sitter's Club*—and has created multimedia products around them. Scholastic is doing in the book business what Disney has done in the entertainment business: Take name-brand franchises and bring them into lots of different markets. *The Magic School Bus* is the best example of this technique. *The Magic School Bus* is a series of fun science books for kids 8–12 years old. These books have been best sellers for the past six or seven years. Out of this series, Scholastic has created a PBS television series that is now the second or third highest-rated children's show on PBS. Each of these episodes has become a home video, and several have become CD-ROMs.

Scholastic is taking the print franchise, bringing it into the video world, and then bringing it into the multimedia world. Not surprisingly, the result is one of the best revenue and growth stories in the business. Scholastic is the best example of where the industry is going. It is the farthest along in leveraging its print franchises, but all the players are looking to do the same thing. McGraw-Hill is starting up a significant multimedia publishing operation. Harcourt General has an interesting joint venture with one of the smaller educational software companies. Houghton Mifflin has introduced a series of CD-ROM titles for the consumer market, which leverage some of its best known trade names, including *Curious George*, the *Peterson Field Guide* series, and the *American Heritage Dictionary*.

Question: Please discuss the product cycle of a title, planning prepublishing costs, and the future revenue streams. Are these revenue streams highly dependent on title releases or curriculum series releases?

Appert: The educational publishing business has a long lead cycle and lots of up-front costs, both of which serve as barriers to entry. A company will take three years and perhaps $30 million to create a new math program. In the case of a reading program, a company could spend $50 million or more. A publisher will likely spend these development dollars in Years 1 and 2 and may not see revenues until Years 3 or 4. That product will then be in the market for about five years, with the capitalized development costs amortized against revenues.

Publishers time their product updates to coincide with major state adoption cycles. As a result, revenues (and costs) are highly dependent on state adoption schedules. Part of the reason for my upbeat view of the prospects for the educational publishers is the very active adoption cycle over the 1997–99 period. This should be the largest three-year period of textbook purchases in at least a decade.

Question: Where do these publications' development costs reside on their balance sheets? What happens when there is a dud on the income statement?

Appert: Typically, publishers capitalize the development costs of a product and start expensing it in the year they start selling the book. The smart publishers will expense the development costs associated with their products very quickly. Typically, though, they capitalize the development costs of a product and start expensing it in the year they start selling the book. Although standards vary, I prefer to see publishers expense these costs on an accelerated basis over three to five years. The reading program or math program a publisher has created should be in the market for three to five years, and it becomes more profitable the longer it is in the market. Harcourt General is enjoying this cycle right now. It has the best-selling math and reading products on the market currently. It has largely amortized development costs for these products and is, therefore, enjoying very attractive margins.

The educational publishers have typically enjoyed fairly stable market shares, implying that "duds" are few. To come up with a product that is going to displace the product a teacher has been using for many years is difficult. The market share shifts that have occurred have been mainly a result of the consolidation process. The disappearance of competitors has created opportunities to grow share and improve margins.

Question: Looking at the online providers of professional, legal, accounting, and medical information, to what extent is their content proprietary and can they resell it?

Appert: Generally, the content is extremely proprietary, and that proprietary aspect is the key to creating profitable online services. If you have something proprietary that professionals need to do their jobs, you can easily justify a premium price for it. An example is McGraw-Hill's Shepard's unit, which is one of the largest legal publishers in the United States with its niche in legal citations.

Shepard's product is clearly applicable to electronic delivery. Electronic delivery not only makes the product more widely accessible (because not every lawyer wants to pay the high subscription price for the complete print products) but also substantially reduces production costs. The physical cost of printing the book and delivering it is quite high, so even if the publisher charges less for the electronic version than for the printed product, the margin on the electronic version frequently can be higher.

Question: Please comment on the magazine business. Is the outlook the same for general interest and special interest magazines?

Appert: Public pure-play magazine companies are few, so investors must participate through distribution companies. I have conveniently sidestepped the magazine business because, from an investment standpoint, there are not too many ways to play it. The magazine business suffers from some of the same dynamics as newspapers: cyclical pressures from paper costs and from a relatively soft advertising environment. Within the magazine business, however, the best approach is to look at the two large segments separately. The consumer magazine business tends to be quite cyclical and very competitive. The trade publishing business and professional magazine publishing tend to be more proprietary and tend to enjoy higher margins. At the moment, consumer magazines are on the same trend as newspapers: a cyclical deceleration in the rate of ad revenue growth.

Question: What should the newspaper companies do with their excess cash flow? Should they buy each other? Should they use it as bait to be acquired by others? Should they do stock buy-backs? Should they invest it back into their product and do more electronic media?

Appert: This issue is critical for the newspaper publishers. A huge disparity exists right now between private and public market values in newspapers: If the stocks are trading at 7 times cash flow, acquisitions are still going for 12 or 14 times cash flow.

Thus, acquisitions are not economically appealing. Given the free cash flow dynamic of the business, the newspaper companies should be shrinking their equity bases. Share repurchases on a short-term basis can be accretive to earnings and, potentially, can work to close the gap between private and public market values. Of course, share repurchases must be undertaken in the context of having to continue to spend the money on product development and maintaining physical plants so that the companies can stay in business. I think more-leveraged balance sheets might be appropriate for many of the newspaper publishers.

Question: Will advertising revenues continue to be a coincident indicator in the future, as they have been over the long term in the past? Where is growth coming from? Is it units or pricing on both the circulation and advertising sides? Has the recent decline been more unit based or pricing based?

Appert: The media business was a significant beneficiary of high inflation rates in the 1970s and early 1980s. Because revenue growth is significantly price driven and less unit driven in the advertising business, the decline in inflation has had negative implications on industry revenue growth. In the future, growth will continue to be largely pricing driven. For newspaper publishers, if ad revenue growth was in the neighborhood of, say, 6 percent in 1995, it was probably 2 percent units and 4 percent pricing. That dynamic is probably similar for the magazine publishers.

Going forward, unit growth in the print advertising business probably is going to correlate pretty well to real GDP growth, and so it will probably grow a couple percentage points a year. Total revenue growth, then, is a function of what you can squeeze out beyond that from a pricing standpoint. Pricing is getting tougher and tougher, certainly in the newspaper business and also in the magazine business, because of the increasing competition from both existing and new media.

Question: What is your opinion of niche or small-market newspapers and shoppers? What is their future, and what are their valuation parameters?

Appert: Small-market daily newspapers have traditionally enjoyed the highest operating margins in the newspaper business. A well-run monopoly newspaper in a small market frequently can earn 30 percent operating margins. A small-market monopoly is a wonderful business franchise, which is probably one of the reasons Warren Buffett—despite all the negative things I have told you about newspapers—still likes this business and still has significant exposure to it. The franchise in a small local market tends not to be volatile. Typically, a TV station will not start up in a place such as Lafayette, California, where I live. No radio station is specific to Lafayette, so the local newspaper captures virtually all of the local advertising other than what goes to direct mail. I do not see the electronic media having much of an impact on that franchise.

The free weekly papers and the shoppers, however, have become more commodity advertising vehicles subject to all the competitive pressures on pricing from direct-mail operators, television, and radio. The commoditization of the weekly and shopper businesses has resulted in a reduction in their margins. That situation is not going to change.

Question: Is circulation price elastic? In other words, should the newspapers start a strategy of cutting circulation prices to get circulation up?

Appert: That is an interesting point. Magazine publishers in the past 10 years embarked on a very specific strategy of shifting more of the burden away from advertisers to readers. Going back 10–15 years, the revenue mix in the magazine business was similar to newspapers today: maybe 75–80 percent advertising driven, and 20–25 percent circulation driven. The magazine business today on the consumer side is roughly 50/50 advertising versus circulation. That situation has reduced the cyclicality of the magazine business and made it somewhat more attractive.

Newspaper publishers cannot get to that dynamic; to do so

would require price increases that would be much too aggressive. The newspaper business clearly has price sensitivity; therefore, the publishers have had to be fairly careful about circulation price increases. The higher quality publications—the *New York Times* and the *Wall Street Journal*, for example—have been able to get away with fairly aggressive price increases and maintain the bulk of their circulation, thereby improving their profitability. The lower quality papers, the papers that spend less on editorial content, have not enjoyed that leverage and have seen a fairly high level of sensitivity between circulation and pricing. Absent increased spending on editorial content, newspapers are going to have a hard time getting circulation prices to a level that would result in a mix similar to that of the magazines.

The Advertising Sector

James D. Dougherty, CFA
Senior Vice President, Equity Research
Dean Witter Reynolds Inc.

> Experiencing its best period in more than a decade, the U.S. advertising industry appears likely to continue this successful trend in 1996. New venues such as the World Wide Web and new technologies such as digital distribution are creating dramatic opportunities as the advertising business evolves from simple promotion to logistical support for clients. Operating expenses are crucial to the valuation of advertising companies.

The U.S. advertising industry is currently in its best period since the early 1980s. Taken together, 1994 and 1995 saw the greatest year-to-year increases in advertising spending since 1983 and 1984. The ingredients are in place for another good year in 1996.

Industry Trends

The growth and future of the advertising business continue to be outside the United States, particularly in Latin America and Asia (excluding Japan). Almost 25 percent of the world's advertising spending currently comes from these two markets, where year-to-year increases continue to run into double digits.

Within the United States, national advertising is growing more rapidly than local advertising, and this trend should continue. **Table 1** indicates that newspaper advertising growth is fairly slow, with a five-year cumulative average growth rate (CAGR) of 6 percent. Because newspaper advertising constitutes about half of all the dollars spent on local advertising, local advertising cannot grow at rapid rates as long as newspaper advertising growth is only about 6 percent a year.

Among the major categories, automotive product advertising has become the most important in the United States. In 1990, 14 percent of national spending was by auto companies, and by 1995, that share had risen to 18 percent. This increase compensates somewhat for declines in retailer spending on advertising. In 1985, about 35 percent of national spending on advertising was for consumer packaged goods. This share had declined to 28 percent by 1990 and then to 23 percent by 1995. One cause for the slow growth of the advertising sector through the mid-1980s and early 1990s was the decline in retail goods advertising, although in 1994 and 1995, growth perked up a little. If that revival turns out to be a secular change, that would be a major positive for the sector going forward.

Unbundled media are the specialist media-buying companies whose only function is to buy media advertising for their clients. They do not perform full-service advertising. Three companies—Omnicom Group, Interpublic Group, and Cordiant—are significant entities in unbundled media. We have done pro forma statements that assume Omnicom owns all of Aegis Group, whereas it currently has a 9 percent stake. If these data were true, however, about 23 percent of these agencies' billings in 1995 would have been from specialized media buying, which carries a lower commission rate of about 5 percent relative to a 12 or 13 percent commission on full service. Specialized buying carries much larger margins than full service, however. That 10 percent of revenue translates to about 20 percent of the operating profit of these agency groups and is a very important dynamic in the future profitability of the business. The expansion into unbundled media buying should be a major factor during the next several years in the United States.

Table 1. Local U.S. Advertising Spending, 1992–97

	1992	1993	1994	1995	1996[a]	1997[a]	CAGR 1992–97[a]
Total volume ($millions)							
Newspaper	$27,135	$28,405	$30,450	$32,430	$34,538	$36,265	6.0%
Television	8,554	9,029	10,177	10,885	11,788	12,614	8.1
Radio	6,725	7,342	8,164	8,815	9,547	10,215	8.7
Yellow pages	8,132	8,287	8,511	8,870	9,402	9,919	4.1
Other local media	4,724	5,007	5,403	5,760	6,267	6,706	7.3
Total local	$55,270	$58,070	$62,705	$66,760	$71,542	$75,718	6.5%
Year-to-year changes (%)							
Newspaper	1.5%	4.7%	7.2%	6.5%	6.5%	5.0%	—
Television	7.1	5.6	12.7	7.0	8.3	7.0	—
Radio	4.9	9.2	11.2	8.0	8.3	7.0	—
Yellow pages	1.4	1.9	2.7	4.2	6.0	5.5	—
Other local media	2.1	6.0	7.9	6.6	8.8	7.0	—
Total local	2.8%	5.1%	8.0%	6.5%	7.2%	5.8%	—

[a]1996–97 data are estimates.

Source: Dean Witter Reynolds, based on data from McCann–Erickson.

Valuation and Price Performance

The price performance of the advertising group is shown in **Figure 1**. Since 1984, agency group stock has moved in parallel with the S&P 500 Index but has underperformed it. The P/E in most periods moves in sync with the S&P 500, but **Figure 2** shows that they diverged in the early 1990s. The agencies' earnings performance during that period exceeded that of the S&P 500. Since that period, S&P 500 earnings have recovered, and the P/Es are again close to being in sync. The price–sales ratio, shown in **Figure 3**, trades in a narrow band. Price is between half and one times sales. This ratio hit some peaks in the 1980s, and it is now pushing back up to trade in the one-times-revenue range again.

The ratio of market capitalization to EBITDA, shown in **Figure 4**, is between 6 and 10. Since the

Figure 2. Advertising Group P/E

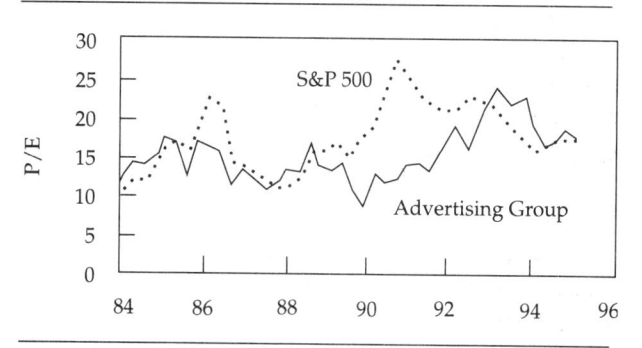

Source: Dean Witter Reynolds.

early 1990s, EBITDA has dipped. One reason for the downward trend is that Omnicom and Interpublic are engaged in fairly aggressive acquisition programs, so their balance sheets carry a lot of goodwill and amortization. Unlike the newspaper companies, agencies are conducting acquisitions at antidilutive prices. That circumstance offers a good buying opportunity because those agency valuations should look for that 10-times-EBITDA number again. A fair amount of money can be made if they do.

Interpublic has been the star investment of this group for many years. As illustrated in **Figure 5**, it has been a significant outperformer almost every year—and certainly on a cumulative basis—since the early 1980s. In almost every year, its ad revenue

Figure 1. Advertising Group Price Performance

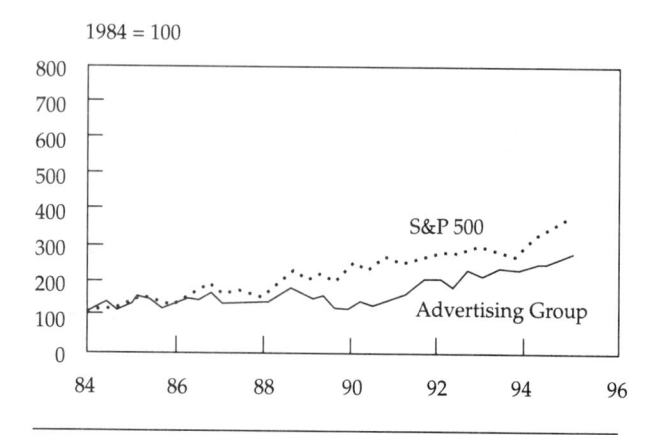

Note: 1984 value of 100 equals year-end closing price.
Source: Dean Witter Reynolds.

Figure 3. Advertising Group Price-to-Sales Ratio

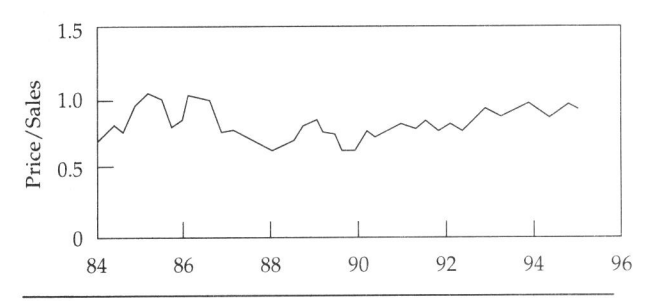

Source: Dean Witter Reynolds.

has grown faster than the average for the industry. The same dynamics are apparent quarterly and by geographic area.

A couple of key ratios are particularly important to the agency business, and according to **Table 2**, these ratios are favorable for Interpublic. Salaries and related expense should be about 55 percent of revenue, and the balance of expenses should be about 30 percent of revenue; about 15 percent goes to operating profit. Operating profit should cover interest by 8 to 10 times. If that happens, earnings per share (EPS) will show steady growth. Keeping the share base stable is important, and Interpublic buys back about $30 million worth of stock a year. The agency's steady growth has led to dramatic outperformance. Our current target price for Interpublic is $51. We take DeanWitter's estimate of the fair value multiple of the S&P 500 (17 times), apply the upper end of Interpublic's relative range (1.2 times) to our 1996 estimate for Interpublic ($2.50), and get $51.

Omnicom was founded in 1986 from a three-way merger. As shown in **Figure 6**, its stock performance was flat from 1986 through 1990, but it has been a dramatic outperformer since then. Because of its substantial revenue numbers, Omnicom has been a dramatic outperformer of the industry each

Figure 4. Advertising Group Market Capitalization-to-EBITDA Ratio

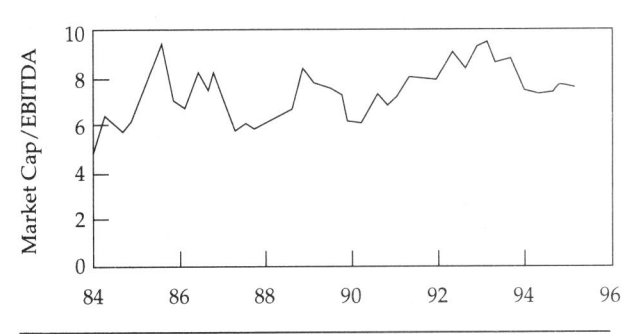

Source: Dean Witter Reynolds.

year since 1990. About one-third of that revenue is acquired. Omnicom stock is trading in the 16 to 17 range, and ample acquisition opportunities exist in the form of small- to medium-size agencies willing to sell in the range of 8 to 10 times net income. As a result of this attractive financial pattern, we expect Omnicom to continue to grow. **Table 3** shows Omnicom's salaries and related costs at about 55 percent and its other operating expenses at about 30 percent. It covers its interest costs by 8 or 10 times. Our target price for Omnicom is $42. Again, we take Dean Witter's estimate of the fair value multiple of the S&P 500 (17 times), apply the upper end of Omnicom's range (1.2 times) to our 1996 estimate for Omnicom ($2.08), and get $42.

Figure 5. Interpublic Price Performance
(versus S&P 500 and agency group)

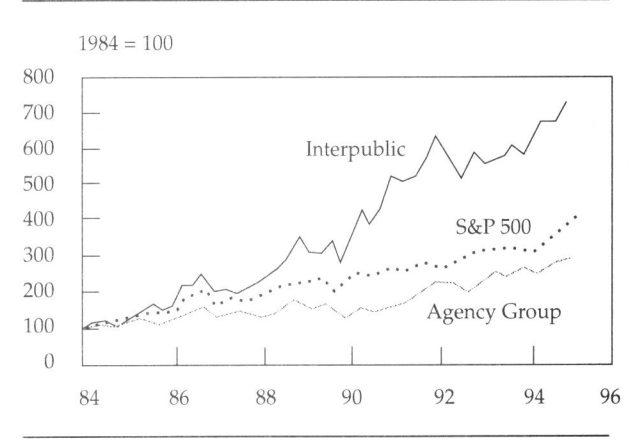

Note: 1984 value of 100 equals year-end closing price.
Source: Dean Witter Reynolds.

At the other end of the spectrum, the next three groups illustrate underperformers. As shown in **Figure 7**, True North Communications' price performance has been below that of the industry for several years and has been trailing off recently. Its revenue performance in comparison to the industry is erratic: ahead in some years, behind in others. It has not had the steady earnings performance of Interpublic or Omnicom. Its margins are shown in **Table 4**. About 63 percent of its revenue goes for salaries and 29 percent goes into office and general, so more than 90 percent goes into operating expenses. It cannot cover its interest costs to anywhere near the extent that Interpublic and Omnicom can, so it does not get the earnings performance or stock performance. We recommend this stock on a value basis. We do not see any reason to look for a premium here, but a market multiple on our estimate for 1996 would still indicate a $25 target price.

Table 2. Interpublic Group Operating Results, 1992–97
(millions of dollars)

	1992	1993	1994	1995[a]	1996[a]	1997[a]	CAGR 1992–97[a]
Revenue	$1,856.0	$1,793.9	$1,984.3	$2,199.2	$2,460.8	$2,668.5	7.5%
Cost and expenses	1,615.6	1,535.7	1,701.8	1,865.7	2,082.0	2,248.2	6.8
Salaries and related	993.1	917.2	1,040.6	1,157.6	1,284.7	1,378.3	6.8
Office and general	622.5	618.5	661.2	708.1	797.3	869.9	6.9
Operating profit	240.4	258.2	282.4	333.5	378.8	420.3	11.8
Interest	33.2	26.4	32.9	38.7	40.0	40.0	3.8
Income before taxes	207.2	231.8	249.5	294.8	338.8	380.3	12.9
Provision for taxes	91.3	99.8	109.0	126.1	145.7	163.5	12.4
Other	–3.9	–6.7	0.7	–0.7	0.0	0.0	NM
Net income	111.9	125.3	141.3	168.0	193.1	216.8	14.1
EPS	$1.50	$1.67	$1.87	$2.15	$2.50	$2.85	13.7
Shares outstanding (millions)	74.6	75.2	75.5	78.0	77.3	76.0	0.4

NM = not meaningful.
[a]1995–97 data are estimates.
Source: Dean Witter Reynolds.

WPP Group, a U.K. company, was a poor performer throughout the early 1990s, as indicated by **Figure 8,** but it is seeing some recovery now. It was strong in 1995 and again (so far) in 1996. Its revenue performance relative to the industry is erratic: ahead in some but not most years. WPP's operating profit margin in 1995, shown in **Table 5**, should have been only 9 percent, which covers its interest by only 5 times. It does not have the steady earnings growth needed for good stock performance. Our target for WPP is $29.

Under U.K. accounting, goodwill amortization does not go through the earnings statement, so the WPP numbers available for analysis are distorted.

Figure 6. Omnicom Price Performance
(versus S&P 500 and agency group)

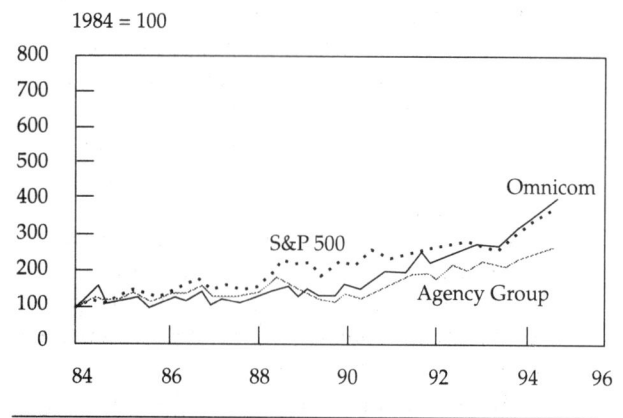

Note: 1984 value of 100 equals year-end closing price.
Source: Dean Witter Reynolds.

We value WPP's advertising revenue at the same rate that we value True North's. WPP contains a substantial component of market research operating profit, which we value at a composite operating profit multiple. We assign no value to WPP's public relations business because it is break-even or loss in most years. Even without that business, the target price is $29.

The real disaster is Cordiant, formerly Saatchi & Saatchi. Since it was turned over in 1988, it has declined, as shown in **Figure 9**, mainly because of its revenue performance. Its three down years—1994 through 1996—came during the best advertising period the United States has had. Cordiant's revenue performance has been both poor and erratic, which shows up directly in its margins, as indicated by **Table 6**. A 4 percent operating profit margin barely covers its net interest charges, so this firm cannot earn anything approaching the returns the other agencies get.

CKS Group had its initial public offering in December 1995 and has been off to a good start since then, as shown in **Figure 10**. That performance should not be any surprise in the light of the revenue comparisons being generated. Such revenue performance is much easier for small companies because the comparisons are relative to the size of the other groups. CKS also has a high-technology application that leads to many of these very favorable revenue comparisons. More companies like this one should be bringing technologies to the business, with equivalent comparisons.

Table 7 shows that in 1996, we expect CKS's

Table 3. Omnicom Group Operating Results, 1992–97
(millions of dollars)

	1992	1993	1994	1995[a]	1996[a]	1997[a]	CAGR 1992–97[a]
Revenue	$1,385.2	$1,516.5	$1,756.2	$2,061.9	$2,284.4	$2,498.1	12.5%
Salaries and related costs	798.2	879.8	1,009.1	1,191.1	1,318.5	1,441.4	12.5
Other operating expenses	433.9	467.5	542.5	620.0	685.3	749.4	11.5
Operating profit	153.1	169.2	204.6	250.8	280.5	307.3	15.0
Interest paid or accrued, special charge	10.1	14.6	11.9	12.0	11.0	9.0	–2.3
Interest paid or accrued	40.9	41.2	34.8	38.1	34.0	25.0	–9.4
Income before taxes	122.3	142.6	181.8	224.7	257.5	291.3	19.0
Income taxes	53.3	59.9	74.3	90.1	103.0	116.5	16.9
Income after tax	69.0	82.7	107.4	134.6	154.5	174.8	20.4
Equity in affiliates, minority interests	0.3	2.6	0.7	–0.7	1.0	2.5	NM
Net income	69.3	85.3	108.1	133.9	155.5	177.3	20.7
EPS (primary)	1.23	1.40	1.57	1.86	2.12	2.39	14.2
EPS (fully diluted)	1.16	1.31	1.54	1.83	2.08	NM	NM

NM = not meaningful.

[a]1995–97 data are estimates.

Source: Dean Witter Reynolds.

---

salaries and related expenses to be about 29 percent of revenue. This percentage is half that of the other agencies, which illustrates what the application of technology to all areas of agency operations can do. Its other expenses are higher, but as the revenue grows and these expenses decrease as a percentage of revenue, CKS has the potential to deliver operating margins in excess of anything the advertising industry has ever experienced. We have a target price of $47. Some part of CKS's revenue is related to doing Web sites, so its valuation gets tied up in the Internet mania. We value that part of its revenue at comparable multiples to Netscape Communications and others. The balance of the revenue we value at other Internet-related but not pure technology plays. We discount the whole calculation at 40 percent a year to allow for the highly speculative nature of doing valuations based on Internet play, but it is still a very strong price target.

Impact of the Internet

The Internet is a major topic of conversation in the advertising business. A study released in October by Nielsen Media Research and CommerceNet (a consortium of companies and organizations interested in creating an electronic marketplace) shows that about 37 million people in the United States and Canada have access to the Internet. That number is comparable to the number of people who had cable TV, VCRs, and telephone answering machines back in the mid- to late 1980s. If Internet usage parallels these historical examples and increases at the same rate between now and the year 2000, Internet penetration will almost double—about 60 million people will have Internet connections.

Of the 37 million people in the United States and Canada with Internet access, 24 million have used it during the past two months. The 18 million

Figure 7. True North Price Performance
(versus S&P 500 and agency group)

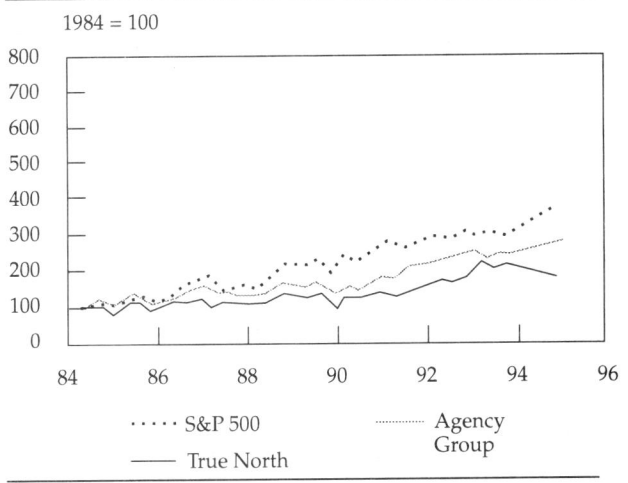

Note: 1984 value of 100 equals year-end closing price.

Source: Dean Witter Reynolds.

Table 4. True North Communications Operating Results, 1992–97
(millions of dollars)

	1992	1993	1994	1995[a]	1996[a]	1997[a]	CAGR 1992–97[a]
Revenue	$353.3	$372.7	$403.7	$437.9	$457.0	$500.0	7.2%
Operating expenses							
Salaries and benefits	204.3	221.0	249.0	273.5	285.4	308.9	8.6
Office and general	103.4	109.3	117.7	127.1	132.6	144.5	6.9
Cost of sales	19.5	8.2	0.0	0.0	0.0	0.0	NM
Provision for doubtful accounts, direct marketing cost of goods sold, unusual transactions, interest expense, other expense	9.5	10.9	1.1	5.7	5.2	5.5	−10.4
Pretax income	16.7	23.2	35.9	31.6	33.8	41.1	19.8
Income taxes	10.9	6.6	16.1	14.1	14.9	18.1	10.7
Income after taxes	5.8	16.5	19.9	17.6	18.9	23.0	31.9
Minority interest expense, equity in earnings of affiliated companies	15.9	9.2	10.3	15.1	13.7	13.8	NM
Net income	21.7	25.7	30.2	32.7	32.6	36.8	11.1
EPS	1.00	1.15	1.34	1.45	1.46	1.65	10.6
Shares outstanding	21.7	22.4	22.7	22.5	22.3	22.3	0.5

NM = not meaningful.

[a] 1995–97 data are estimates.

Source: Dean Witter Reynolds.

World Wide Web users are a key target for businesses. They are upscale, professional, and well educated; the predominant age group is 25–45 years. The Nielsen/CommerceNet study found that approximately 2.5 million people bought something through the Web.

The most important element in getting significant money to flow to World Wide Web advertising is a credible third-party measuring system. We believe that system will be the joint venture of Nielsen Media Research and Internet Profiles Corporation (I/PRO). Nielsen has the sampling in place—25 countries, 75 meter panels, more than 50,000 households, and 100,000 meters—to measure a population-projectable sample of all households, whether Internet-connected or not. I/PRO has several advantages. It is skilled in doing research on World Wide Web audiences. It has passive registration—through its I/CODE universal registration system—by which the user of the Web registers once, thus avoiding registration at multiple sites. It has one password that controls the level of information each user is required to deliver. From this configuration, the content providers get demographic data without affecting the traffic on their sites. The data collected include age distribution; income level; gender mix; easy-to-understand individual preferences; and importantly, aggregated audience data across the sites, which is a crucial difference between what I/PRO is doing and what some other research companies are doing on the Web.

I/COUNT is a product of this joint venture. I/COUNT analyzes visits at a Web site, not simply "hits"—that is, not merely the number of times a site and its resident pages are accessed. It determines frequently accessed files and directo-

Figure 8. WPP Group Price Performance
(versus S&P 500 and agency group)

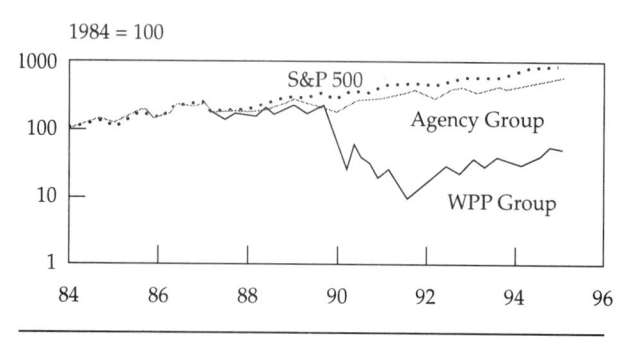

Notes: Index is based on logarithmic scale. 1984 value of 100 equals year-end closing price.

Source: Dean Witter Reynolds.

Table 5. WPP Group Operating Results, 1992–97
(pounds in millions, except as noted)

	1992	1993	1994	1995[a]	1996[a]	1997[a]	CAGR 1992–97[a]
Revenue	£1,273.4	£1,426.7	£1,426.9	£1,542.1	£1,626.8	£1,716.3	6.2%
Operating profit	70.8	95.0	112.1	136.9	161.0	168.0	18.9
Net interest charge	34.1	29.8	26.8	27.3	25.4	22.0	−8.4
Non-operating exceptional items	−28.9	−10.9	0.0	0.0	0.0	0.0	NM
Income before taxation	7.8	54.4	85.3	109.6	135.6	146.0	79.6
Provision for taxation	17.2	29.4	35.8	44.9	55.6	59.9	28.3
Minority interests	2.5	2.1	2.1	1.8	2.3	2.4	−0.5
Preference dividend	0.0	2.4	1.1	0.0	0.0	0.0	NM
Attributable to shareholders	−11.9	20.6	46.3	62.9	77.7	83.7	NM
Earnings (loss)/ADS[b] Fully diluted	$−0.90	$0.53	$1.04	$1.36	$1.67	$1.80	NM

Note: Exchange rate: £1.00 = $1.55.

NM = not meaningful.

[a]1995–97 data are estimates.
[b]American Depository Shares.
Source: Dean Witter Reynolds.

ries, names, geographic distribution, and industry codes and can compare the site with a benchmark of industry standards in I/PRO's data base. Being able to compare across all the sites and across other media is critical. When combined with I/CODE, I/COUNT gives good site-usage information that can be merged with demographic profiles of visitors.

The advertising agencies and advertisers will want to see third-party audits before real money starts to flow. These audits show visits per month, average visit length, visits by day/week, time of day, most frequently accessed sites, and visitors by organization names. Such information constitutes the beginning of a credible third-party system, which should be essential for traditional media budgets to start flowing to the Web.

Figure 9. Cordiant Price Performance
(versus S&P 500 and agency group)

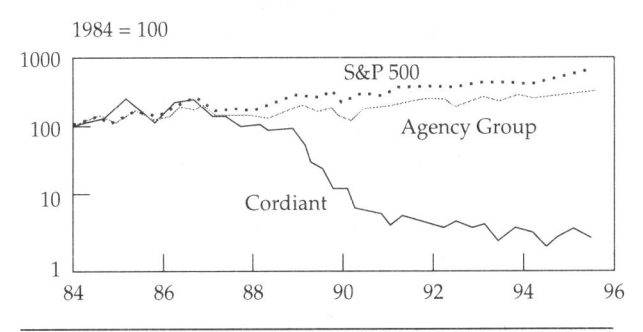

Notes: Index is based on logarithmic scale. 1984 value of 100 equals year-end closing price.
Source: Dean Witter Reynolds.

New Technologies in Advertising

Technology is also being used in other ways in advertising. WPP Group's advertising firm, Ogilvy & Mather, for example, used digital animation for Shell Oil. The objective of the commercial, which features dancing gasoline pumps and cars, was to put a little fun into buying gasoline. Gasoline is a low-interest product, and digital animation puts some excitement into it. The production house is R/Greenberg Associates (R/GA). Robert Greenberg is one of the fathers of digital production in the advertising business. The technique is motion capture, in which the original performance involves human dancers connected via cables and sensors to a computer. The animation is done over those images so that the pumps and cars move just the way humans do. This technique is very dramatic and adds a lot to the creative process.

Cordiant's Saatchi & Saatchi advertising firm made some interactive disks for the Toyota Tacoma pickup truck. The objective was to appeal to leading-edge consumers (people who are buying trucks as recreational vehicles). The disks attempt to maintain the pleasant aspects of buying a new vehicle while minimizing the need to visit dealers. Another element is to enable Toyota to deliver a corporate public relations message. This

Table 6. Cordiant Operating Results, 1992–97
(pounds in millions, except as noted)

	1992	1993	1994	1995[a]	1996[a]	1997[a]	CAGR 1992–97[a]
Revenue	£731.2	£806.0	£775.4	£734.7	£712.0	£761.8	0.8%
Operating and administrative expenses	661.4	728.2	705.2	661.0	635.0	667.2	0.2
Depreciation	25.2	29.2	25.7	26.0	26.0	26.0	0.6
Severance and reorganization	–10.0	–19.1	0.0	–20.1	0.0	0.0	NM
Property provisions	0.0	2.3	0.0	0.0	0.0	0.0	NM
Operating profit	34.6	31.8	44.5	27.6	51.0	68.6	14.7
Net financial expense	17.7	12.6	13.4	25.1	8.0	8.0	–14.7
Disposal of subsidiaries	1.8	–3.6	1.3	–26.8	0.0	0.0	NM
Discontinued operations	–13.8	3.6	0.0	0.0	0.0	0.0	NM
Total pretax profit	4.9	19.2	32.4	–24.3	43.0	60.6	65.4
Income taxes	13.4	10.6	14.6	12.0	15.5	21.8	10.2
Net shareholders	–8.5	8.6	17.8	–36.3	27.5	38.8	NM
Minority interests	5.2	1.3	3.9	2.7	2.8	3.0	–10.4
Net ordinary shares	–13.7	7.3	13.9	–39.0	24.7	35.8	NM
EPADS($)[b]	–0.38	0.17	0.29	–0.82	0.26	0.38	NM
ADS[c] outstanding	56.4	66.1	73.4	73.8	147.7	147.7	21.3

Note: Exchange rate: £1.00 = $1.55.

[a] 1995–97 data are estimates.
[b] Earnings per American Depository Share.
[c] American Depository Shares.

Source: Dean Witter Reynolds.

promotion went out last June or July with a very modest print campaign, and Toyota had 70,000 requests for disks. The disk can be used in any computer, in interactive kiosks, and on the Web. It contains everything customers need to know about buying a car. For example, in case people think Toyota is a Japanese car company, this disk is designed to remind them that Toyota has many

Figure 10. CKS Price Performance
(versus S&P 500)

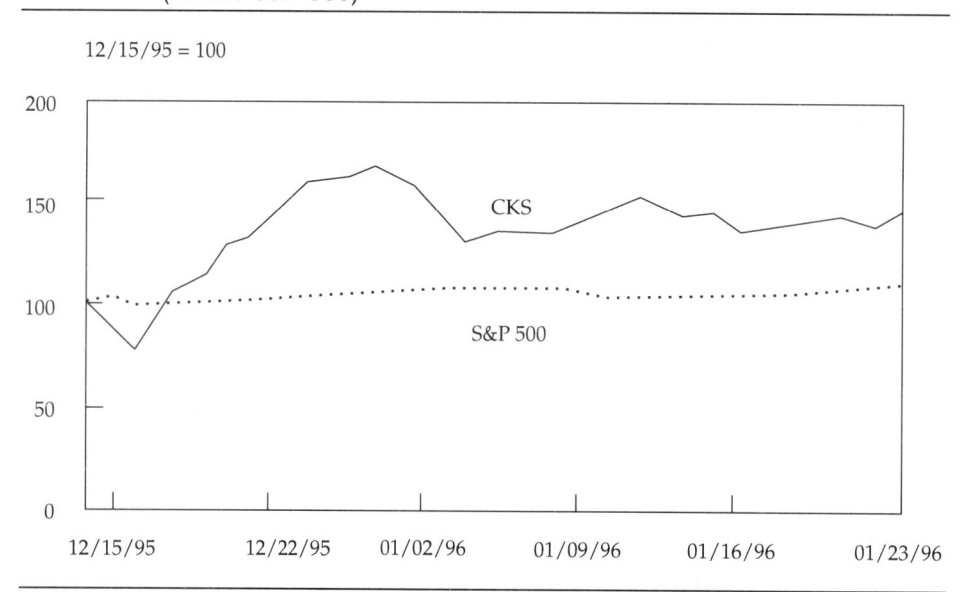

Note: 1995 value of 100 equals closing price on December 15.
Source: Dean Witter Reynolds.

Table 7. CKS Group Operating Results 1993–98
(thousands of dollars)

	1993	1994	1995	1996[a]	1997[a]	1998[a]	CAGR 1993–98[a]
Revenue	$12,038	$22,938	$34,792	$52,000	$70,200	$94,770	51.1%
Operating expenses							
Salaries and related	2,782	6,168	10,485	14,979	20,358	26,920	57.5
Other operating expenses	6,183	11,121	13,164	18,996	25,974	35,065	41.5
General and administrative	2,584	5,131	8,688	12,214	15,479	20,500	51.3
Operating income	489	518	2,455	5,811	8,389	12,285	90.6
Other income (expenses)	–25	–38	–27	2,437	2,656	3,042	NM
Pretax income	464	480	2,428	8,248	11,045	15,327	101.3
Taxes	185	192	1,062	3,505	4,694	6,514	101.7
Net income	279	288	1,366	4,743	6,351	8,813	100.9
EPS	$0.03	$0.03	$0.13	$0.37	$0.49	$0.68	113.8
Shares outstanding	8,482	9,944	10,726	12,727	12,900	12,900	—

Note: Data are for year ending November 30.

NM = not meaningful.

[a]1995–97 data are estimates.

Source: Dean Witter Reynolds.

production facilities in the United States that employ a lot of U.S. workers. If they click on any of those sites, the disk tells them exactly what is done at the facility, how many people are employed there, and who the union shop steward is. If they look at a vehicle and click on "calculate," it tells them how much it is and what their monthly payments would be. Basically, customers are ready to go to the dealer with a completed price form.

The classified newspaper advertising business is worth about $13 billion a year. Help-wanted advertising is about $3 billion annually, half of which is collected by help-wanted agencies and half by the media. Bernard Hodes Advertising billed about $380 million in 1995—12 percent of the total. Hodes is part of Omnicom Group's Diversified Agency Services (DAS), and it works off a Web site called CareerMosaic. The first item is a job reference list. The listings come in from job seekers who fill out the form online. The form is immediately posted on the job reference list, which changes constantly. Job seekers can also post their resumes on the site for employers to hit.

Most of the use of the Web for job seeking and filling openings is done by high-technology people, but that situation is changing. The CareerMosaic help-wanted software has doors that users can open—employment products, news, overview—to see what is inside. It shows all of the firm's products. When people click on those doors, they get all the technical specifications. Engineers and other high-technology job applicants can go forward to another level that brings up all of the recent press references to that firm. People doing research in preparation for an interview can go into this function and download all that information. The company also gets a chance to present its mission statement, history, location, and culture.

This capability should transform the help-wanted business, because the economics are dramatic. A one-month listing on CareerMosaic costs $150—for a site that generates 5 million hits a month and 3,000 searches a day. The equivalent exposure in a local newspaper would cost more than $1,000, so a listing with CareerMosaic costs less than 15 percent of what it costs to do the same thing in a newspaper. Bernard Hodes is a major buyer of help-wanted media. It has the customers, and the media costs on the Web are trivial. The newspapers may start bringing their help-wanted advertising to Bernard Hodes, rather than vice versa. Some smaller papers already are. Companies such as Hodes that latch on to this technology and get up on the Web should have the opportunity to become substantially bigger businesses in the future than they have been in the past.

The distribution of audio commercials is now becoming digitized. Digital Generations Systems (DG) is one company that has started in this direction. These listings show what is currently being spent to distribute spot advertising, new single releases, network advertising, syndicated programs, and news. More than $200 million is spent simply to distribute radio material. DG's revenue is a small fraction of that amount. A large amount of money can be made this way. The benefits are obvious.

Digitally distributed commercials cut four hours from the current system, and they offer perfect accountability, positive confirmation for every spot being delivered, full reliability, and a single point of responsibility from start to finish. They also provide CD-quality sound, as opposed to third-generation analog tapes.

R.R. Donnelley & Sons Company's digital division is an example of digital distribution of print advertising. Advertisers need to reach smaller audiences with shorter print runs, faster time-to-market requirements, and increasingly, support of logistic rather than strategic initiatives. Donnelley's location is adjacent to the Federal Express hub in Memphis, Tennessee. Advertisers transmit digital files to Memphis that go directly to digital presses with no platemaking or film or anything in between. Files sent by noon go out with Federal Express that same day. This system creates a virtual printshop anywhere in the United States.

Donnelley is running a case study with the Service Merchandise retail chain. Service Merchandise reports data from every sale in every store to a data base maintained by Donnelley's digital division. Every Sunday, these data are compared with the sales data base, and individual promotions are created and mailed every Sunday night. For example, if a store is overloaded with camcorders, the system searches, finds all the customers that bought a VCR in the past six months at the store, and sends them a specialized promotion offering a camcorder at 20 percent off.

The advertising process is shifting from merely promoting goods to helping clients solve logistical problems. For the first time, Donnelley is in the $40 billion short-run print business. That amount is two-thirds the size of the commercial printing business as a whole. Donnelley has become a $6 billion company overall, so this business, unlocked by applying digital technology, has enormous upside potential.

The last example is AdValue Media Technologies, an interactive network that connects media representative firms, agencies, and stations. Among the advantages it offers are reduced credits, online invoicing, resolution of disputes, and faster payments—plus no lost orders, no rewriting or retypesetting, and no disputes. Free spots for sales credits in the spot television business amount to 1 percent of spot billings a year, an estimated $20 billion in 1995. One percent of that amount is $200 million—solely from eliminating disputed spots. AdValue has in place the first nationwide network. Its revenue is a very small percentage of $200 million, but the use of its service is growing rapidly. It started in 1993 and placed $143 million worth of spot that year and $515 million in 1995; its estimate for 1996 is about $1.5 billion.

A typical television station might have $100 million in billings and carry 60 days in receivables. Assuming a 10 percent interest rate, if that receivable carrying number gets cut to 30 days, the station's savings in cost of money in receivables is about $700,000. The station can also eliminate $500,000 in sales credits and save more than $100,000 in order-processing costs. So, AdValue can add $1.3 million to the EBIT line of an average television station. With 1,500 television stations in the United States, the savings soon add up to real money. The interesting part is that Reuters is listed as a 50 percent owner of AdValue.

Conclusion

The rules of the new technology call for redefining value in an economy in which the cost of raw technology is plummeting toward zero. Sooner or later, this plunge should obliterate the worth of almost any piece of software. Then, value will lie in establishing a long-term relationship with customers.

Are we heading for a period in which we are going to have a real-time transaction market for advertising availability, much as we do for stocks and bonds? In my opinion, yes. Advertising comes in widely accepted trading blocks—pages, lines, 30-second spots, and so forth—just as stocks and bonds do. The value of these blocks varies in time according to market conditions in the eyes of the beholder. The tendency of media buyers to believe they are smarter than the next person provides a real incentive for the development of a real-time market. Such a transparent system would limit abuses of the black-box system—particularly in non-U.S. countries where such abuses have been a big issue. I believe we are moving in this direction, and within five years, we will see it happen.

Question and Answer Session

James D. Dougherty, CFA

Question: Can you give us a sense of the timing of widespread advertising on the Internet? How will other media be affected?

Dougherty: By the year 2000, advertising on the Web should be roughly equivalent to that on national cable television, or $4.5 billion. The event that needs to take place is the development of credible, third-party audience measurement. That development is underway and probably will be completed within the next year. The media that would be affected most would be those that are moving toward small audiences and individual communication, such as direct mail marketing, the national yellow pages, and national spot television.

Question: In the future, do you see advertisers moving more toward bulk buys or targeted buys? In other words, please provide a sense of the future of television versus the Internet versus print and other media.

Dougherty: I do not see much incremental money coming into the advertising stream. U.S. advertising looks to be a growth business in the range of 6–7 percent a year. We estimate it will be $174 billion in 1996. Growth of 6 percent on $174 billion will not change much. The money that goes to the Internet will come out of other media. I am not looking for large incremental additions of money into the total advertising pool.

Consider the triviality of the media costs on the Internet. In September 1994, you could put up a half-decent Web site for $45,000; in September 1995, the cost was $150,000. Some of the real heavyweight sites cost more than $1 million. The cost escalates as more content goes in. That expense is really all there is. A $500,000 garden variety Web site is the same cost as the production of a 30-second commercial for network television. Each $500,000 in production that is spent in the U.S. advertising industry in the year is multiplied up to $4.3 million worth of media. The $500,000 spent on the Web site might cost $20,000 a month to keep up for a year. If the third-party audience-measurement device says that the two are equally effective in selling your products, advertisers should rush to the Web, because the $500,000 does not have to be followed by $4.3 million in media buys.

Question: Will the ad agencies be the intermediaries with this rush to the Web?

Dougherty: They had better be. I have said many times that the only institution in the history of the world that is as reactionary as a large advertising agency is the medieval Roman Catholic church, but even it eventually came around to the printing press. The enabling event for the Internet was a speech by Edwin Artzt, then CEO of Procter & Gamble, at the American Association of Advertising Agencies in May 1994. He said, "This is happening, and if you do not get in the game, you are going to be out of business." That speech started a major runaround of activity in the advertising business. Virtually every major multinational publicly traded group tried to get into the game. Most of them do not have the skills under their own roofs to do it, and so entities such as CKS are turning up and being invested in, by Interpublic in this case. Such companies are going public at big prices, a prelude to many more of them yet to come. You will see a lot of specialized high-technology agencies coming into the business, and they will be welcomed with open arms.

Question: Are commission percentages going down, and are commissions on new media higher than the traditional media?

Dougherty: The various agencies have a myriad of commission arrangements. Interpublic and Omnicom probably have hundreds of different payment arrangements with their clients. Mostly, the payment is done on the basis of a commission rate plus a bonus for achieving certain goals. If you take both Interpublic's and Omnicom's actual billings worldwide and compare them against the actual revenues reported, the percentage is 14.5 percent—very close to the old 15 percent, despite a lot of concern expressed during the past 10 or 15 years about that commission deteriorating. Two of the biggest, most demanding, and most sophisticated clients—Procter & Gamble and Coca-Cola—still pay the full 15 percent. The clients with the greatest need for sophisticated advertising and the most knowledgeable buyers are willing to pay the full freight.

Question: How do you determine relative premiums to the S&P 500 for your valuation purposes?

Dougherty: I use historical data. In 1983 and 1984, the agency group hit 20 percent premiums to the market. We have been waiting for

The Media Industry

them to get back to that ever since, and this is probably the year they are going to do it.

Question: What characteristics do you need in order to be positioned for the foreign markets? Should you be starting up new agencies or acquiring foreign agencies?

Dougherty: Most foreign growth has been through start-up offices established many years ago. More recently, to build their volume, the agencies have been filling in those start-up agencies with acquisitions. Also, the agency groups that did not participate have historically found it necessary to do acquisitions.

Question: Do you expect the advertising companies to use their excess cash to continue the consolidation of smaller agencies or to buy back their shares?

Dougherty: The financial dynamics of the advertising business dictate that companies acquire agencies. Omnicom seems to have the formula down best. Its growth is significantly higher than the industry average. About one-third of that growth represents companies acquired at antidilutive prices—that is, Omnicom can buy an agency at about half of its earnings multiple. Many good small- to medium-size agencies are willing to sell for 8 to 10 times net income. As long as a company's stock is priced at 16 or 17 times, an acquisition of 8 to 10 times is a very attractive proposition.

On the share buyback, to keep EPS growing at decent rates, you need to keep the share count constant. Both Interpublic and Omnicom, which are the two major acquiring companies in the group, buy back enough stock to keep the number of shares more or less equivalent. For example, Interpublic has bought back more than 12 million shares of stock in the past five years, which has almost offset all the stock it put out for acquisitions and for various employee plans and options. Keeping that share count constant is a very important part of Interpublic's financial objective.

Question: Promotions siphoned off advertising dollars in the five years prior to 1993. Has this trend reversed in recent years? Can you comment on whether people will start doing more promotion again?

Dougherty: Measured media have slowed down because the data are accurate and widely available. The data on promotional activity are highly suspect. I am not sure people can tell where that money went. To say that it went to a promotion is convenient, but I am not sure of that assessment. The packaged-goods companies would like nothing more than to get back into general advertising, which they believe is the best way to build their long-term brand franchises. That approach is subject to a lot of countervailing pressures, particularly trade pricing pressures. This situation is why I mentioned that the packaged-goods business bounced back reasonably well in 1994 and 1995. I hope that marks a secular return of the packaged-goods companies to advertising growth, but I am suspicious. This may have been a bounce-back recovery that will prove to be an exception rather than the rule going forward.

Changes in the Industry Dynamics

Christopher P. Dixon
Managing Director
PaineWebber, Inc.

> The media industry is at the nexus of fundamental changes in the way people receive and use information. The confluence of new distribution technologies, the emergence of new international markets, and shifts in the demographic and psychographic profiles of the typical media consumer have changed the game. Internal dynamics are a way to distinguish firms that can be valued through modified dividend discount or growth models and firms that should be valued on a sum-of-the-parts or leveraged buyout basis.

A fundamental structural shift began in the late 1980s as the media industry started to consolidate. That consolidation was driven first by efforts to create scale economies to take advantage of new distribution technologies and, second, by raw fear. The fear was that new technologies and markets would pass companies by and that media companies would need to build a critical mass of diversified product lines to become less reliant on mature businesses while developing a broad enough operating base to minimize the risk associated with moving into new markets. Today, this structural evolution can be seen in the television industry. Networks, station groups, and cable system operators are all grappling with a shift from the analog distribution of video alone to the digital distribution of video, voice, and data.

Much the same thing is now occurring in traditional publishing. Newspapers are looking to expand and develop electronic delivery systems to make up for a declining circulation base in their traditional franchises. How media companies deal with these shifts is going to determine the structure of the industry tomorrow. Before we look forward, let's take a step back and see how we got to where we are today.

In television, the ability to access relatively low-cost capital in a low interest rate environment, coupled with a regulatory shift resulting from a recognition that the rules were no longer appropriate to a changing industry dynamic, has fueled the formation of a de facto oligopoly. This year's capstone merger between the Walt Disney Company and Capital Cities/ABC was the topper and a tacit acknowledgment that the days of "big media" are upon us.

Big Media

Today, there are five global media companies—News Corp., Disney, Time Warner, Tele-Communications Inc. (TCI), and Viacom. In addition, two communications megagiants—General Electric and AT&T—are sniffing around the periphery and a variety of smaller "niche" players or big media "wannabes" such as The Seagram Company, Westinghouse Electric Corporation, and Sony Corporation. Increasingly, media has become a global oligopoly, with very real barriers to entry created by the need to generate high levels of internal cash flow and maintain a low cost of capital.

On the macro level, we have also seen the development of what has been referred to as a communications *kereitsu*. News Corp. has joint ventured with TCI and MCI; Disney has ongoing relationships with a variety of telephone companies; AT&T recently invested with DirecTV; and Time Warner, despite a nasty suit with U S West, continues to negotiate with a variety of larger telephone providers. Microsoft wants to get into bed with everybody. The recent agreement by NBC to offer news as part of Microsoft's package of online services is another example of the trend. Each of the major companies is experimenting with online communications services, trying to be part of the network-centric personal computer universe of tomorrow.

In addition to the global players, there is an emerging pack of local media operators, ranging from large quasi-local enterprises, such as the *New York Times*, to small individual radio stations. Here, the successful model has been to think global and act local—protect the franchise while looking to build a national brand. The success of the national edition of the *New York Times* or global editions of the *Wall Street Journal* comes immediately to mind. And once again, we have seen a variety of experiments in new media, such as the *Nando Times* and the *New York Times* on the Internet. Companies are investing time and money to establish a beachhead in the interactive electronic world of tomorrow.

The fundamental business model of the media industry today is similar to that of the newspaper and broadcasting sector over the last 50 years. Buying a media property is no longer sufficient; look to increase advertising and circulation revenues and make efforts to control labor and distribution costs. The trend for the latter half of this decade appears to be joint ventures that access differing skill sets and allow the firm to move into new markets and delivery platforms as they become established.

Today, a media company first needs to identify and then learn to compete with a whole host of new players, ranging from online news services to satellite-delivered subscription television. No longer are only one or two competitors in the market willing to share revenues, each knowing that it is only a matter of time before the pendulum swings and one gets its turn as the market share leader.

Today, the market is fragmented, and once that share is gone, nothing guarantees that it will ever return. In essence, the biggest problem for U.S. television networks is market fragmentation. Share for the three largest networks is now down to 52 percent of television viewing, and in the youngest demographic group—kids—personal computer use now surpasses television use. The business is riskier, and a company first needs to protect its core franchises as it looks to experiment in new ones. Once a company loses that franchise, it may never get it back.

Vertical Integration

One way companies are seeking to reduce risk is to vertically integrate. The risk inherent in the production of television programs and the fragmentation of the market has forced companies to own at least one distribution channel. The theory is that the producer can create long-term incremental library value for a program by using the channel to launch and promote the project. This is a very big part of the rationale behind the Disney/Cap Cities and Time Warner/Turner Broadcasting System mergers. Note that one of the key details in the Disney merger was that Capital Cities granted Disney the right to program the Saturday morning ABC lineup. Turner Broadcasting's various networks also provide, at minimum, a guaranteed outlet for Warner's vast array of television programs.

The best example of vertical integration in the media industry has been in television. The fundamental industry structure shifted dramatically in response to an altered risk profile and increased fragmentation. What happened in television over the past 10 years may be viewed as a model for what will occur as media in general begin to focus on an increasingly fragmented customer base, which may lead to vertical integration.

Ten years ago, the syndication market and three-network model proved a very efficient way of sharing the inherent risk of a capital-intensive business dependent on the whim of the public. In those days, a network executive knew that the cost of licensing most programs for two airings would be covered by advertising fees and that a few hits a season would account for network profits. The producers were willing to deficit finance and take relatively low license fees because the promise of syndication could easily offset the risk of the flop—witness *The Cosby Show* or *Dallas*, which generated hundreds of millions of dollars for the producers.

As program costs rose and overall network ratings declined, the industry risk profile began to change. *Home Improvement* or *Cheers* could still generate sufficient revenues in syndication to offset the production deficits, but fewer and fewer network programs could generate sufficient off-network fees to make up for network deficits. Station managers with low ratings in a fragmented world conserved programming budgets. They were still willing to pay for top-rated shows but increasingly resorted to barter for the less established programs, and few producers were able to take barter to the bank.

This situation led to the joint ventures formed by ABC and DreamWorks SKG, the recent deal between NBC and New World Communications Group, and the development of the United Paramount Network (UPN) and the Warner Bros. network (WB). In the DreamWorks deal, the idea is to share the risk, minimize the impact of escalating costs in the third year of a show's success, and have the producer and network share advertising revenues in the later years. The net result is to minimize deficits by keeping costs under control and allow the producer to share in a portion of the network revenues. On the flip side, joint ventures such as that between NBC and New World allow the network to share in the back end. At the UPN and WB networks, the idea is to guarantee day and date distribution of first-run syndication programming and, at the same time, build a new branded network.

At the core of each model is a response to the increasingly fractionalized market for television programming and recognition that, for the vast number of network programs, the business model no longer worked. It was a good model. For almost 20 years, it provided a way for networks to offer new programming at a cost below production and provided producers a way to receive sufficiently high returns to offset the risk of a show not making it to a second season. A hit such as *Frasier* or *Friends* can still generate more than $100 million in off-network license fees, but the majority of this year's new sitcoms will be unable to recoup costs from North American syndication rights.

The point is that if television is the model for what happens when a particular medium fragments, a proliferation of distribution channels across all media will force companies to come up with innovative solutions to share the risk associated with manufacturing media content and may result in increased industry vertical integration.

The New Media Consumer

The shift in the way consumers use and receive information also has startling repercussions. Today, a breaking news event is first released on CNN, followed by a news wire report. The news weekly of yesteryear has become an executive summary of the week's events. Compare *Time* magazine of today with that of the early 1950s, and the change is startling. The array of choice for an advertiser has expanded also. With the success of Viacom's networks—MTV, VH-1, Nickelodeon—and with CNN's viewership during the Gulf War and the O.J. Simpson trial, advertisers have finally recognized cable as an effective way to expand their reach. Early experiments with the World Wide Web by online news services such as Nando.net and advertisers such as General Motors and MCI suggest that once someone figures out how to measure the audience on the Internet and charge for it, the proliferation of choices is going to expand yet again and a new medium will come of age.

In a sense, Marshall McLuhan was right—the medium is the message—and the challenge for media companies is to make sure that the information they are providing and charging for is being presented in the medium best adapted to the individual message. Increasingly, the editorial decision will not be whether something goes on the front page or is buried in the back of the book but whether that information should be released to a particular user group electronically before being included in the daily edition. This change may have startling repercussions, as indicated by the recently announced joint venture between NBC News and Microsoft. NBC journalists, for example, will now be reporting stories to be posted on the Internet at the same time they are preparing for the *NBC Nightly News*. Another NBC joint venture with Intel allows for the simulcast of data and programming to customers who can view television on their personal computers, allowing orders to be placed for products that are being hyped by Jay Leno's guest on *The Tonight Show*.

From a financial perspective, these ventures in new media can result in greater efficiency and generate significant incremental revenues with relatively little additional cost. In the Microsoft/NBC venture, whereas NBC previously maintained a news operation to produce only 30 minutes of *NBC Nightly News*, it now has continuous output through a variety of distribution channels that can generate incremental revenues against the same fixed operating costs. In the Intel venture with NBC, the incremental revenue streams also result in enhanced value for the network as a promotional and advertising vehicle; and for newspaper companies, once a certain level of critical mass is reached, online services should be able to generate cash flow margins approaching 75 percent.

From a strategic perspective, the biggest challenge will be how each company in this industry will use its current media platform to expand and develop new sources of revenue while seeking to protect its position in an increasingly competitive market for information. At Time, for example, each of the company's magazines is increasingly viewed as a source of everything from special editions to CD-ROMs to television programs. Witness the ubiquitous Martha Stewart or the wide variety of *Sports Illustrated* special editions. This ability to generate incremental revenues by introducing brands across a variety of media platforms will become increasingly important as the market for information continues to fractionalize and narrow-casting begins to displace broadcasting.

Media Model Number One: Content Is King

To date, the communications businesses have had only two basic business models. In the first model, or "library model," a company owns a proprietary data base, archive, or program library and is able to license that product to a variety of users for differing fees based upon the medium used to deliver the proprietary product. This model assumes that license fees are then reinvested to create, update, and refresh the library or data base and thereby continue to attract new users.

Historically, the best example of this model has been in the music or film business. The emergence of the compact disk and video cassette helped offset the impact of rising production and promotion costs in recent years. One of the more intriguing structural shifts is how this model will translate to information businesses, such as the magazine and newspaper industries, as consumers become more comfortable with electronic, online delivery systems and as further communications standards are developed. Note also that this model is the basis for the interest in "content" expressed by so many media analysts. The theory is that the company that manufactures content will receive annuitylike cash flows over a long period of time as new delivery mechanisms require product to fill an empty distribution window.

In fact, this model is really a spillover from the model of the mid- to late 1980s in the film industry. There, the emergence of British Satellite Broadcasting and Sky Television (since merged into BSkyB), combined with the establishment of the video cassette and the coming of age of HBO, created huge new sources of previously nonexistent revenues. As demonstrated by Michael Eisner with Disney and Ted Turner with Turner Broadcasting, owning a library of more than 200 hours of programming would create significant barriers to entry to other competitors and (in Turner's case) generate sufficient cash flow to help rebuild highly leveraged balance sheets.

Interestingly, a corollary of the so-called content model—and one cause for concern—is that on an individual project basis producers now justify higher production budgets with the expectation that they can make it back in the newest window. In film or television, for example, the days when a producer would look to the video window or syndication as "gravy" are long gone. Today, the typical film production is only justifiable based upon the net present value of the stream of cash flows that can be realized from all venues on a global basis over the life of a project. One risk for many media industry companies is justifying capital outlays today based on market expectations that may not develop.

Many of the seeds for today's changes were first planted in the mid-1980s as managements came to recognize the importance of owning a library of motion picture and television programs and the ability to exploit new distribution technologies and tap previously underserved markets, particularly outside the United States. The merger of Time with Warner Communications, the purchase of Columbia by Sony, the investment of Matsushita Electric Industrial Company in MCA, and the merger of Viacom with Paramount and Blockbuster were to various degrees predicated on the idea that owning a library and a manufacturing capability was the road to nirvana. In television, this need to own programming was a leading driver behind the demise of financial syndication rules, which when combined with loss of network hegemony, set the stage for the latest round of media mergers—the combination of Disney and Capital Cities and the pending merger of Turner Broadcasting and Time Warner.

One of the more intriguing investment themes will be the degree to which information and publishing companies emulate the consolidation of the 1980s as new delivery mechanisms such as the Internet and high-speed modems create new sources of revenue for news and information providers. If one thinks of the *Wall Street Journal* or *USA Today* as a huge repository of data and manufacturer of information in a user-friendly format, the opportunities become apparent.

Recently, the focus on building libraries has shifted to developing libraries of brands. In television, the trend has been to build format-specific branded networks such as Viacom's MTV, Nickelodeon, or Lifetime; Time Warner's CNN, the Cartoon Network, or HBO; and Disney's ESPN or the Disney Channel. In each case, the strategy has been to build an identity around a programming format that is easily differentiated and has a defined demand, whether it be for movies, news, kids' programming, or sports.

The theory is that a specific brand first will have pricing power among advertisers that target a specific consumer and, second, will provide a way into emerging multichannel television markets. An established brand can also act as an important platform to experiment in new media developments—witness the Internet promotions of Warner Bros. and the ESPN home page on the World Wide Web.

Recently, Edgar Bronfman, Jr., chairman of Seagram, noted that one of the unique aspects of the media and entertainment business is how quickly a brand can be created. He noted, for example, that Seagram took almost 15 years to introduce Crown Royal into the United States but Universal took less than 60 days to introduce and establish *Jurassic Park* on a global basis. One of the challenges for Seagram (as was the case for Coca-Cola during its foray into the media industry) will be how to adapt its broad-based consumer marketing skills to introduce media brands in emerging countries such as China.

Media Model Number Two: Distribution

If content, the development of proprietary franchises, and the building of brands has been one model, the other approach to operating media franchises has been to expand, develop subscriber bases, and capture fees based on customized offerings—in other words, to get paid for being the gatekeeper. In its ultimate permutation, gatekeeping is the economic basis for Time Warner's full-service network (FSN) in Orlando, Florida, and the source of much of the modeling going on in the cable business today. Gatekeeping is also the model behind suburban or local editions of major newspapers.

Having subscribers requires a distribution system, however, and keeping them requires the ability to provide and market custom offerings across the network—hence the latest media buzz word "bundling." Bundling is the driving force behind AT&T and MCI's moves into satellite delivery of video. The idea is to provide bundled video, data, and voice services in order to hold on to current customers in the face of emerging competition and to develop new business lines.

Importantly, the battles among transport mechanisms—be they wired, wireless, or cable—are beginning to disappear with the received wisdom of the day, suggesting that although a hybrid fiber coaxial (HFC) system appears to be the most robust transport mechanism with the highest bandwidth, a place remains for wireless, satellite, and telephone transport. The battle lines are being drawn across scale, because a transport company needs to be large to generate sufficient revenues to amortize the cost of the network. The concept of four large companies transporting branded content on a global basis on a broadcast, satellite, wired, or wireless platform has intellectual appeal and may become reality. Should that happen, be prepared for another paradigm shift in which distribution is viewed as more important than content in the way this industry is structured and valued.

In an ideal world, the structure should break down functionally, with telephone and cable operators first focusing on providing a robust broadband network infrastructure that will be able to carry voice, data, and video. The architecture should be open, allowing for the entry of a wide variety of electronic equipment suppliers to offer high-speed modems, digital set-top boxes, servers, switches, and a variety of customer-premises equipment. All systems would be interoperable and standards would be truly global; competition would be driven by product offerings and marketing. But that is a perfect world, and as those who have watched the cable industry know, it can only occur "in your dreams."

Still, the challenge during the next several years will be to build the infrastructure to stay ahead of the demand for new services while adapting to the more complex world of information and two-way communications. Nowhere will this battle be more apparent than in the rush to offer high-speed modems. The world of high-speed data transport is relatively virgin territory and is one of the few places where a level playing field exists for all competitors. If cable operators—in conjunction with equipment manufacturers such as Hewlett Packard, AT&T, Intel, and Motorola—can seize the high ground in high-speed data transport, they will fundamentally change the structure of the industry. They will break the equipment oligopoly represented by General Instrument Corporation and Scientific-Atlanta, alter the customer base of those companies, and force them to change the way they serve their customers and upgrade and rebuild plant.

The first out of the blocks usually wins the race. The first to market can create important competitive advantages. When working with new technology, the natural tendency is to put off what can be done today until tomorrow, when it will be cheaper. In the long run, that delay can be very expensive.

For example, Wall Street and the financial press have largely written off Time Warner's experiment in Orlando as a bust, citing the expense and the lack of FSN subscribers. But what is less clearly understood is the enormous importance of what Time Warner is learning by being first to market. The experience gained in everything from finding out how long it takes to design robust network load-management systems or how to handle customer inquiries about a broad array of services can have significant implications as the digital world matures and as Time Warner upgrades its plant on a nationwide basis. Comcast Corporation's recent announcement of its plan to hire college graduates as service representatives able to answer questions on everything from a monthly bill to "how do I configure my computer with your modem?" underscores the steepness of the learning curve and the importance of being first.

Many of the larger software and hardware manufacturers and operators will have a natural tendency to create proprietary software applications that can become industry standards and generate incremental cash flow from licensing agreements. But as Lotus so clearly discovered with Lotus 1-2-3, the killer application of spreadsheets, today's killer application can die or be mortally wounded tomorrow. Thus, TCI's efforts with its @Home Network may prove for naught if another cable operator is able to align with Yahoo! (a Web site that provides users with a guide for the Web and the Internet) and Hewlett Packard to create user-friendly, bundled high-speed access to the Web. Bundling translates to cross-promotion and cross-marketing, again creating a natural advantage for the large, vertically integrated operators such as Time Warner, Comcast, and TCI/Liberty Media and helping to fuel the *kereitsu*like structure of the industry.

Regulation

One big issue, which we hope is behind us, has been regulation. From a public policy point of view, concentration of power is a very real concern, and from a corporate point of view, there are real needs to expand into new areas to justify the expense of upgrading facilities. Essentially, the battle lines have been drawn, on the one hand, by a company's desire to amortize the capital costs of creating state-of-the-art communications networks and, on the other hand, by governmental concerns about all consumers having equal access without monopoly pricing. In telecommunications, size matters. Once the network has been built and the fixed costs expended, each incremental customer generates incremental profit. And from a government point of view, a community of communications-literate haves and communications-illiterate have nots can, at the very least, be destabilizing. The passage of the Telecommunications Act of 1996 will create an appropriate framework to address these issues, and everybody can get back to business.

Capital

One other factor that has led to today's industry structure has been the need for external capital. This business is capital intensive. Whether for upgrading a cable system, producing a dramatic television series, or acquiring a music library, the business eats capital. In cable, this need has translated to relatively highly leveraged capital structures, whereby management looks to use interest and depreciation to optimize the firm's ability to deploy internally generated cash on a tax-efficient basis. In entertainment, and with the Disney/Cap Cities deal, a focus on optimizing capital structures has led to creating a larger company with a more leveraged balance sheet and lower average cost of capital or hurdle rate.

Today, the industry has undergone consolidation, has a significantly lower cost of capital than at any time in recent history, and is poised to benefit from scale economies, emerging international markets, and a bewildering array of new technologies that help people communicate and share information. The industry is peopled with entrepreneurial managements—exemplified by Sumner Redstone, Rupert Murdoch, and John Malone—who minimize natural tendencies to become bogged down in bureaucracy and interdepartmental battles. Most importantly, the industry is made up of cash-flow-producing franchises that are extraordinarily difficult to replicate.

What Is Next: Managing for Growth or Investing in the Pieces

Looking forward, the big challenge for management will be how to structure the firm internally to ration capital and maximize shareholder returns while taking advantage of a cornucopia of opportunity. Right now, two models are emerging. The first is best exemplified by Viacom or Disney, and the second is best represented by TCI and its various entities. For purposes of securities analysis, the internal dynamics should also be viewed as a way to differentiate between, on the one hand, firms that appeal to traditional growth managers and can be valued through modified dividend discount or growth models and, on the other hand, firms that should be appropriately valued on a sum-of-the-parts or leveraged buyout basis.

At Viacom, the strategic focus has been to integrate a diverse array of businesses to a common culture driven by budgets and cross-promotional opportunities. Viacom is the only firm in the media industry that has an executive vice president of technology who operates across all corporate divisions and has an active role in developing new business. The idea is very simple: Take the core brands and use cross-promotional and emerging technology to create new sources of revenue. Maintain a focus on shedding businesses that do not allow a dominant competitive position or that require high levels of maintenance capital expenditures that can severely hamper the firm's ability to remain flexible and gain first-to-market advantage in new business arenas. At the end of the day, the goal is to create a global media brand, which can be as ubiquitous as Coca-Cola or Phillip Morris and generate explosive levels of cash. A newly rationalized Disney/Cap Cities also fits this mold.

The other model is being developed at TCI. Fueled by 20 years of capital-raising experience, the plan calls for breaking the company into autonomous operating units. Importantly, the individual businesses can be self-financing, and securities issued at the individual operating level can be used as acquisition and joint venture currencies. A significant point is that this model is particularly suited to the telecommunications industry, because it allows for low-cost financing of infrastructure costs through double leverage (both the holding and the operating company and at the subsidiary) and is based upon the relatively stable utilitylike cash flows. It also provides enormous flexibility in the face of local regulation because it enables management to play "hide the pea," something that any of us who have watched the formulation and reformulation of Liberty Media uniquely appreciate.

Importantly, this structure of loosely interconnected nation states allows TCI to enter into a variety of joint ventures and thereby lower the risk of moving into new businesses. At TCI, the two best examples of this structure are the "triple play alliance" with Sprint and other cable partners, which will enable TCI to move into offering national telephone service on a shared basis, and the TCI/Liberty international alliance with News Corp. both to bid for sports rights and offer sports programming on a global basis. In both cases, the alliances allow TCI to use companies with a more established presence to carve out an early-stage position in a potentially lucrative field.

These internal structural differences can drive valuation methodologies. In the first case, for companies such as the new Disney or Viacom, investors will use traditional growth methodologies to determine value. The key focus should be on cash flow growth and the ability to generate top-line growth in a variety of economic scenarios. In the second model, as investors look to alliances formed among leading cable companies by Time Warner or News Corp., analysts will need to value the sum of the parts and adjust for the ownership claims represented by the public entity.

At PaineWebber, we take the analysis one step farther by looking at expected equity returns relative to the market and applying a combination of a discounted cash flow analysis and the DuPont model. We use EBITDA as the key input, because it represents the firm's ability to internally generate and grow cash and is a way to compare companies with highly differing capital structures, capital expenditures, and dividend requirements. Our models currently project that the sector is expected to generate an estimated compounded annual return on equity of 20 percent—at the low end of historical ranges but consistent with an industry in which cash flow is projected to grow by 11 percent and which is levered at slightly more than four to one. Importantly, the current leverage ratios also translate to an industrywide average cost of capital or internal hurdle rate of 14.6 percent, a relatively low historical level that can allow management to pursue acquisition strategies to boost internal returns and fuel further industry consolidation.

Opportunity Knocks

What is next? In our view, the next phase of industry development will be driven by how the major media companies (1) expand into new international markets and (2) learn how to use the rapid development of network-centric personal computing to further leverage traditional media franchises. Importantly, this evolution is not hardware driven. Whether information is retrieved through a computer, a hand-held device, or television has little meaning for most media companies, because individual appliances will be developed to meet consumers' demands. In the digital age, information will be increasingly platform neutral, as a PC in the kitchen with recipes on CD-ROM and wide-screen satellite-delivered television in the living room become the norm.

Anyone who has seen today's 13-year-old kids surf the Internet will realize that unlike the past decade's teens who were entertained but somewhat sedated by television, today's kids are invigorated by the pace and abstract nature of the World Wide Web. Most importantly, by the time the infrastructure has been completed, those kids will be in their early 20s.

Fundamentally, the media business is expected to continue to benefit from two revenue streams: subscription or direct sales, and advertising or indirect sales. From a macro level, advertising should continue to grow as a function of GDP. Direct sales, however, will grow in line with the shifts in emerging delivery platforms. As always, analysts will have concerns about cannibalization as they worry about what impact the introduction of a recordable digital video disk will have on the video cassette market. The good news is that, historically, new media such as the compact disk in the music industry or home video have been additive to industry revenues and have resulted in positive returns to those companies that could adapt. Thus, news of the death of video may be premature.

Today, the most interesting potential delivery platform is the Internet and World Wide Web, the world's first shared global local area network (LAN). Today's Web looks as much like the electronic network of tomorrow as yesterday's Osborne computer looked like today's Pentium-based lap top. George Schlukbier—founder of *Nando Times*, one of the first successful online newspapers—recently summed up the situation by saying, "We are two years into a 10-year plan where we targeted our key customers as 18–20 year olds, but our most successful consumers are now 13 year olds. I guess we are on track. We just have to grow up with them."

The business model has yet to develop, with promotion being the primary economic rationale for most Web home pages. A proliferation of computer modems and higher-speed access in late 1996 is expected to accelerate development of business models. Current expectations call for a model similar to cable television, with one fee charge for a basic service and à la carte charges for premium services. Just because this model is early is no reason to dismiss it. My colleague Bill Drewry, who covers the newspaper business, believes that newspapers are in Year 2 of a 100-year business and that the Internet is going to drag newspaper companies and investors kicking and screaming into the modern age.

On the international front, most media companies are probably early, as distribution infrastructures need to be built before cash flows can be generated from program licensing. Demand is real, as evidenced by total international sales for motion pictures, which on a specific-project basis now outpace North America rentals. For example, MGM's latest Bond picture, *GoldenEye*, has generated $100 million in North America and more than $200 million in other countries. Steps by Rupert Murdoch to expand his satellite reach to encompass South America and, now with MCI, to North America or efforts by Liberty to gain shares of programming assets serving 1.2 billion subscribers in aggregate also attest to the importance of globalization.

From a structural point of view, we expect the media industry to continue to evolve in response to the shifting dynamics of the way people communicate using technology. Successful companies will be looking to take advantage of new technology, increased global demand for information and entertainment, and development of new multichannel video platforms. All media companies will develop and market products that appeal to the psychographic and demographic shifts created by the acceptance of a network-centric personal computer. Internally, companies will also have to become increasingly horizontally structured and will have to push decision making down to the local divisional level, because the response speed in the emerging communications universe requires more fluid and less bureaucratic structures. In publishing, for example, an online newspaper is never "put to bed" and needs constant updating. This advance requires a different management approach.

Rationing capital will be critical, and those companies with proven ability to generate capital internally will have a distinct advantage as the communications infrastructure of the next century develops. The need to respond quickly should put significant premiums on companies with flexible, underleveraged balance sheets.

We expect to see a further bifurcation between "big media," those companies looking to develop global franchises for their mix of brands and products, and local media companies with strong niche positions and a targeted local expertise. Skill in adapting to developing digital standards can also provide unique strategic advantages for content producers and information manufacturers.

The ongoing debate about appropriate levels of regulation will continue. We hope that rules will be established that will allow management to develop long-term strategic and financing plans, as opposed to gaming the regulation of the year. This type of regulation will be particularly important in emerging global economies where copyright protection and franchise ownership are often only theoretical notions.

Also, look for joint ventures to continue to rule the day, as a way both to game regulations and to spread the risk associated with early-stage ventures. The Liberty/Fox/TCI international sports alliance, the NBC/Microsoft news alliance, and the Viacom/PolyGram Records/MTV Asia alliance are important models because they establish the next stage of the communications *kereitsu*. This model will become an industry standard. If it works, expect more.

One big question for the near term will be how the industry digests the acquisition activity of last year. Viacom has already shed some of its noncore assets, such as Madison Square Garden, and plans to spin off its cable operations and Spelling Productions. Depending on the tax ramifications, look for Disney to shed some of Capital Cities' publishing assets and Time Warner to simplify its capital structure once the Turner Broadcasting acquisition has been successfully closed.

Conclusion

Media companies are expected to continue, on the one hand, to rationalize operations and build their core franchises, whether manufacturing entertainment product, building branded networks, or expanding and upgrading distribution infrastructures. On the other hand, companies will look to share the risk of moving into new markets and new technologies by entering into a variety of joint ventures and "going to school." In all cases, the management will be expected to reinvest and maintain relatively high returns on internally generated funds, as shareholders come to recognize that the media firms represent one of the few ways to invest in the dynamic shifts occurring in the ways human beings communicate.

It will be an exciting time, and like the farmer who found it difficult to remember that his primary mission was to drain the swamp when he was up to his neck in alligators, investors may lose sight of their goal. At the end of the day, however, media companies are uniquely positioned to take advantage of the dramatic shifts that are occurring.

The current formation of big media is a natural response to the need to access low-cost capital and take advantage of the rebuilding of global communications infrastructures. The current oligopolistic structure should enable the major participants to protect their positions, as new distribution systems become established. An increased focus on marketing and the recognition that the interactive world of the late 1990s may require internal structures that are less hierarchical than those created by the consolidation of the past 10 years can differentiate the winners and losers. Those companies that focus on their unique capabilities, look to use new technologies to broaden their markets, and do not try to be all things to all customers should continue to post above-trendline growth and generate high returns for shareholders and investors.

The Internet and expanded LANs will have a huge impact on the media universe of tomorrow. Investing in the Internet in 1996 is like investing in radio in 1925, one year before RCA bought out AT&T and formed NBC and two years before a fellow by the name of Bill Paley, who later formed CBS, began to buy advertising for his father's cigar company on a radio station in Philadelphia. The Internet will evolve along a similar path as broadcasting has. Current efforts by AT&T, MCI, Microsoft, TCI, and News Corp. are setting the stage to offer easy access to digitally transported data, video, and voice information. By the end of the decade, four private data broadcasters will emerge that will bundle and package branded content on a global basis to a broad array of personal computing devices around the world.

It is an exciting time for investors and for media companies. The train is just about to leave the station. The challenge for the media industry and for analysts and investors is not to be left behind.

Question and Answer Session

Christopher P. Dixon

Question: What is the brand in the firm business? Is it the distributors, such as Disney and Warner Bros.; is it talent, such as Kevin Costner; or is it the series, such as the James Bond films?

Dixon: In my view, the brand is the project. The project is the entity that you are going to invest in and that then has the life to be able to generate recurring revenues over time. *Star Trek*, for example, is a terrific brand. It was basically developed as a television series and has led to seven movies. Out of that brand, you can now go out and buy a CD-ROM that puts you in command of the starship *Enterprise*. It has been a good brand. Another brand would be Disney's *Toy Story* or Universal's *Jurassic Park*. *Jurassic Park* started as a movie, and now a wide variety of games and merchandise are based on it. In addition, a theme park is being developed by Seagram in Florida. So, the brand is a project or an idea that has the potential for a long-term life and can generate cash flows over time.

Question: Is NBC cannibalizing its own primary market by selling its news product to Microsoft, thereby reducing the potential audience at 7 o'clock? Or does NBC think, "If we do not do it, someone else will?"

Dixon: The real issue is to recognize the different customer base. The startling statistic is that younger people—particularly 13–15 year olds—are not using television or newspapers as their traditional news media. From NBC's point of view, the computer is a way to capture a market that is currently not being reached and at the same time to spread the costs associated with news gathering across a variety of new sources of revenue. So, it is not cannibalizing. Right now, NBC is going after a specific market that is underserved and is not responding to what is being offered in the marketplace today.

Question: Are you arguing that the data bases of news and information held by publishing companies are similar in value to the programming and film libraries of the production companies? Is the comparison of news to entertainment justified in light of the time-sensitive nature of news?

Dixon: I am not sure that the library value is correct. To stretch the paradigm a bit, what we are really talking about is the unique ability to have a news organization that is already formatting and working with information. The Nando.net is something you all should examine, if you have not seen it. Nando is the *News & Observer* in Raleigh, North Carolina. It is owned by McClatchy Newspapers. Forty percent of the people who use it are from outside the United States. It gets about 7.5 million hits a week right now. It has advertisers. It digitally recreates the local newspaper. Not only do the reporters write the stories for the local newspaper, they also write and update the story for the online version. The value is not so much in the library as in the ability to create a very sophisticated format that is user friendly and can be updated easily. A fascinating aspect of Nando is that George Schlukbier, who runs it, happens to have a master's degree in library science. This skill is not from journalism. He knows where to put stuff so that you can relate one thing to another. Think of Nando as a big card catalog and you get an idea of what the Internet really is.

Question: You cited TCI, Time Warner, Viacom, Disney, and News Corp. as dominant players of the future. Does this mean that smaller companies in this sector will become obsolete?

Dixon: One of the ongoing battles is about being global versus local. The big guys can go global, but the little guys know the local marketplace. So, the challenge for many of these smaller companies, particularly television and radio groups, is going to be having a dominant local presence that has the support of the local community. Those companies—whether newspaper, television, or radio—are clearly going to succeed. The other question is what happens to the guys in the middle? Some of them will be bought out, but clearly, some businesses have niche opportunities and dynamics. Medium-size companies, such as King World Productions and Gaylord Entertainment, are large investable vehicles, but by the same token, they have very clearly defined niches that are just a little too small or a little too big for somebody to come in and buy. At the same time, they are large enough to generate significant sources of cash and to have a good business dynamic. You have to be careful. You have to take a look at the local side, and you have to look at those companies that have truly definable niches, whether syndication for King World or country music cable networks for Gaylord.

Question: Twice during your presentation, you stated that four global entities will emerge, but you never said who they will be. What does your crystal ball say about who they will be?

Dixon: This is the big question. I urge any of you who want to get an idea of what is going to happen to go back and take a look at the history of radio from 1922 to 1930. It is one of the most interesting periods of time. The chaos that was going on reads exactly like what is going on in the Internet today. You had companies such as Western Electric, AT&T, and RCA and entrepreneurs such as Bill Paley all looking to seize an opportunity. The four or five companies starting to shake out now are clear and will be defined across transport platforms—broadcasting, telephony, cable, and satellite. In telephone, AT&T will have a presence. There will be a satellite consortium that looks very much like the MCI–News Corp. consortium. News Corp. has the global distribution system; MCI is moving into areas with data. TCI is going to make a play and will be the primary nexus of the cable operators. This group is going to be based upon what is going on with the Sprint grand alliance and is a model for what will be happening and how we see that model develop. TCI has global capabilities. It has access to Liberty, and it has this communications *kereitsu* that exists around the planet. The fourth one is going to be GE–Microsoft. It is the traditional broadcast model that exists today. Right now, its long-term position in sports is phenomenal. It has the Olympics through the year 2011. Next year, NBC will generate more than $1 billion in cash flow. Put that in perspective with CBS and you have to ask, "What did Westinghouse buy?" Those would be the four if I were to pick them, but the real answer is *kereitsu*. To pit one or two players against one another is probably oversimplified. Few big industries can support more than four main players on a global basis, which is why I think four players will dominate. There may be a lot of local guys we do not even know about right now, but the concept is to start thinking about how important and global this arena is.

Question: Can you comment on the positioning of some of the non-U.S. players such as a Pearson, Bertelsmann, or Thompson?

Dixon: We have yet to see significant in-roads by many of the foreign players, with the notable exception of News Corp., into North America. They have not been able to get involved in television production or content manufacturing, and most of them have had difficulty breaking into North America. I would expect to see licensing arrangements. You might be able to go into Germany, for example, with Bertelsmann or the Kirch Group. Many of those companies could function as joint venturers or affiliates. For example, United International Holdings has 12 million cable subscribers in Europe. Very few people are aware of it. A small percentage of it is owned by Philips Electronics, and TCI also is an investor. So, it is a natural affiliation. TCI would have a product that it might offer through an affiliate relationship to United International Holdings. At this point, these companies are probably going to be U.S. based. After the foray the Japanese made in Hollywood, however, we are probably not going to see many non-U.S. participants playing on the global level.

Question: Why do we see some telecom players, such as AT&T, getting involved in direct broadcast satellite (DBS) while others, such as the RBOCs (regional Bell operating companies), venture into MMDS (microwave or wireless cable)? Will some mix different delivery systems in their bundled offerings?

Dixon: What it comes down to is bandwidth. About two weeks ago, I was at Cable Labs. One of the big questions there was: Is the cable infrastructure actually the most robust delivery structure? It comes down to physics. Basically, a 6 megahertz bandwidth cable is a pipe. It is robust, it can be controlled, it can be shielded, and it is two-way. So, there is no question that—in terms of delivery of voice, data, and video—a well-engineered network built with HFC cable has a fundamental technical advantage. Notwithstanding HFC's positive aspects, MMDS has real advantages in places such as western Ireland or Argentina. Western Ireland has more sheep than people, and it costs a lot of money to drop wire through the hills; Argentina has a lot of cattle—same situation. Different platforms will develop, but broadband capability suggests that cable has the advantage.

Telephone does not know much about video. These companies need to go to school to learn about delivering a continuous service. Many of the telephone companies have moved into wireless cable as a way to go to school and learn how to be in that business. Over time, they are either going to migrate into a cable overbuild or they may buy out cable operators. Satellite is a little bit different business. It is tough to justify the payment MCI recently made—$688 million for a Ku-band license business—if you think it is only going to be a video platform. We are talking about spectrum. We are talking about the ability to take that spectrum and configure it in such a way that it becomes digital high-speed data, as well as video. Under that model, personal computers have a full Ku-band digital path downstream and a path upstream to a cellular telephone. The satellite business strikes me as much more a battle for spectrum and for the use of certain products as they are developed than it is a move into video.

Question: Can you discuss the risks of vertical integration? Does this vertical integration create inbreeding and bureaucracy?

Dixon: One of the things that Viacom has done is to combine three significant businesses through vertical integration. Think of Paramount as the manufacturer, the Viacom networks as the packager, and Blockbuster as the distribution system and you get the idea. The jury is still out. Most of the vertical integration has been driven by the idea that content is king and the development of VCR, cable, and the international markets. Distribution is going to become more important, however. Operationally, it is problematic. These companies have very different cultures, and that is one of the key areas that I, as an analyst, will be looking at very carefully.

Question: Regarding the global programming market, is the U.S.-based programming the most valuable, or are we going to see more and more local-based programming, such as the Hong Kong Film Company?

Dixon: American film has the Number 1 or Number 2 market share in every country on the planet. In television, you have to be specific. In South America, people watch three things—soccer, soccer, and soccer. Sports is all important. In parts of Germany, people watch soccer, soccer, and soccer. Local sports has tended to be the Number 1 programming around the world. Filmed entertainment, an American product, has been Number 2, and sometimes, it is the primary market.

Question: Cable has eroded the big three networks during the past decade or two. Could DBS wireless cable or RBOC overbuilds do the same to cable in a shorter period of time?

Dixon: When we are talking about cable, are we talking about video or are we talking about a transport mechanism, which is video, voice, and data? Much of the theory behind the Telecommunications Act is that by allowing cable operators into the local loop, you will be able to create lower access costs for the long-distance businesses. Yes, video can be cannibalized. The pricing will be driven down toward commodity pricing, but the issue is how quickly the cable operators can move to take the first-to-market advantage, either for high-speed data or for competitive access lines. Right now, Cablevision Systems Corporation on Long Island has a closed fiber optic loop through which it is introducing telephony services on Long Island. Cablevision is currently doing business telephony, and it expects to do residential trials by midyear. Those revenue streams from telephone should begin to offset some of the cannibalization that is going to occur coming into the video business. Another example is Rogers Communications in Canada, which is the first company to be able to offer high-speed data transport. In November 1995, they introduced a high-speed modem, and it had 2 percent penetration in the system the first week. Now, the company has a backlog and is getting first-to-market advantage and learning a lot. No question, competition and more commodity-like pricing are coming to the traditional video businesses.

Question: Can you envision the creation of more DreamWorks in the future as creative people feel constrained within the "Big Five" giants?

Dixon: No. DreamWorks is unique. You have three individuals who generated an estimated 70 percent of the industry profits over the last four years. Nobody else has been able to do that. Steven Spielberg, Jeffrey Katzenberg, and David Geffen have acted as a magnet for talent. They have the infrastructure, and they have the operating systems. We think they are going to be very successful. This year, Amblin Entertainment, which had been Steven Spielberg's company and is now what DreamWorks has become, was responsible for *The Bridges of Madison County* and *Casper* and is currently doing the animated version of *Cats*. Its two big films went through Universal and Warner Bros. It is hard to get a hold of that much capital to build that base and, given the lack of consistent performance by most players in the industry, I cannot think of any individual who would be able to establish or compete with something like DreamWorks.

Question: With the great amount of capital expenditures being made by these companies, whether in distribution or content, will they generate a return on their invested capital in excess of their cost of capital? In other words, will these companies make sense on an economic-value-added basis?

Dixon: For equity holders, you bet. As most investment is only incremental, companies are able to generate significantly higher returns on investment from new revenue streams. In the United

Kingdom, for example, adding telephone to a cable plant requires a 50 percent increase in plant but generates 100 percent incremental cash flow.

Question: In the long run, is the idea correct that the Internet favors content versus distribution with respect to the ability to maintain prospective margins?

Dixon: Yes, if the content is cost-effectively updated on a regular basis. This is not the video model, in which you are redistributing a previously produced product; it has to be customized.

Question: With DBS already digital, dish prices falling, data transmission around the corner, and MCI and AT&T linking up with satellites, is cable in danger of losing a big multichannel distribution edge?

Dixon: The industry is becoming more competitive, but the HFC platform provides cable with a real opportunity to be first to market with many of the new revenue businesses.

Question: What is the future for newspapers? What strategic moves are available to newspaper companies?

Dixon: They can use the Internet to leverage their brands and editorial and production capabilities, or they can focus on local markets.

Question: Do cable and telcos ever work together?

Dixon: Yes. On an operating basis, U S West is working well with both Continental Cablevision and Time Warner, and each of the cable companies can build relations with the interexchange carriers.

Question: Given that many new and alternative media brands have come from outside traditional players (i.e., not the networks), how successful will these traditional players be at developing new branded media going forward? Also, will they truly be able to simply transfer their content onto a new medium as you suggest, or is a more costly adaptation or development of a new paradigm more likely?

Dixon: At the end of the day, the new paradigm will be a combination of new and old players, but the traditional media companies that know how to put out a daily paper or news show do have experience and skills that are transferable. At heart, the Internet is a medium, not a technology.

Broadcast and Cable Television Sectors

Andrew W. Marcus, CFA
Managing Director
Alex. Brown & Sons Inc.

> The broadcast and cable television sectors are experiencing a fast-paced period of change in which companies are seeking the critical mass necessary to be competitive. The main events driving stocks in these sectors are changes in regulation of ownership, cash flow growth, and private market values. Analysts should focus on a company's underlying growth and how its management views excess cash.

Media is a growing and exciting industry with many competitive advantages, especially for U.S. companies. In fact, some observers are predicting that media/telecommunications will be the second largest U.S. industry, behind aerospace, by the end of this millennium. In general, most media companies, being in a non-capital-intensive industry, generate excess cash when they are doing well. Thus, when analyzing the media/telecommunications industry, the focus must be on both internal growth and the strategic use of free cash flow. What do they buy? What do they sell? Do they recapitalize their balance sheets? These analytical decisions are certainly as important as the underlying internal growth. So, the industry is a challenge for analysts. Often, analysts cannot go by the numbers only; they must also understand the vision.

This presentation covers the stock market perspective of broadcasting and cable stocks: what drives them, the competition for viewers, the advertising environment, and sector overviews for television broadcasting, radio broadcasting, wired cable, and wireless cable.

Stock Market Perspective

Our belief at Alex. Brown is that stock prices are event driven. Typically, the events driving prices of broadcasting and entertainment stocks are changes in regulation of ownership, cash flow growth, and private market values.

What Drives the Stocks

Regulation is the most important of the three. Regulatory shifts tend to be secular. Growth is not only absolute growth but growth relative to Wall Street's expectations. If a company grows 30 percent but the collective wisdom of the analysts was that the company would grow 40 percent in that particular period, often the stock would trade down. Private market value would enter the picture if, say, a company is in trouble but has an attractive group of assets; the stock trades more on the underlying asset value than on the company's operating characteristics. During the past few years, several media companies have traded that way, the most recent being CBS.

Valuation is like a pendulum. Many stocks are overvalued, and many stocks are undervalued. An overvalued stock can as easily become more overvalued as undervalued; the pendulum can swing either way. There are different schools of investing, and many people make a lot of money saying something will become more overvalued. Just because a stock is overvalued does not mean it cannot double or triple in value if the company exceeds expectations.

As **Table 1** shows, television stocks have outperformed the market for the past three years, along with radio broadcasting stocks. The basic reason for this overperformance is regulatory relief. These two sectors have benefited from looser government restrictions. In addition, their cash flow growth has exceeded expectations. Cable operators and cable programmers have underperformed for two of the past three years. Regulatory uncertainty and reregulation of cable multiple system operators (MSOs) caused them to fall below some cash flow projections. Wireless cable did well in 1995 because the regional Bell operating companies (RBOCs) entered that field and started taking ownership stakes in some of the fledgling companies.

Table 1. Broadcasting and Cable: Stock Price Performance

Medium/Index	1996[a]	1995	1994	1993
Television	21.6%	58.9%	21.6%	60.2%
Radio	23.6	60.4	3.4	107.4
Cable MSOs	NA	19.7	−32.0	38.7
Wireless MSOs	NA	45.6	−39.2	−15.2
Cable programmers	NA	18.3	−19.8	182.6
DJIA	10.1	33.4	2.1	13.7
S&P 500 Index	7.9	34.1	−1.5	7.1
Nasdaq Composite	17.8	39.9	−3.2	14.7

NA = not available.

[a]Data are as of May 17.

Source: Alex. Brown & Sons.

Competition for Viewers

Seventy percent of all viewing is still of programs from the traditional broadcast stations. That 70 percent is down from 85 percent 10 years ago. A vast majority of viewers receive those signals through cable, but they are watching the stations that originate over the air. The audience share for the three networks—ABC, NBC, and CBS—has declined from 66 percent to 48 percent in the past 10 years. The independents and Fox have improved from 19 percent to 22 percent. The three networks have lost a big portion of their share to Fox, not simply to cable. The share for basic cable has improved from 12 percent to 30 percent. Premium cable has held steady at 6 percent.

Some new competitors are coming on board. Direct broadcast satellite (DBS), C-band, and Ku-band have grown rapidly and now reach more than 4.5 million homes. Wireless cable and satellite master antenna (SMATV) each go to slightly fewer than 1 million homes. These new competitors, from which about 6 million households in the United States receive TV signals, will grow dramatically in the years to come.

Today, 72 percent of all U.S. households receive their TV in a paid form, such as cable, DBS, or wireless cable. Only 28 percent use the rabbit ears on their television sets. In the year 2001, only 20 percent of all homes will receive television for free. We believe cable will see a slight decline in its household penetration, from 66 percent to 59 percent; DBS will double, from about 5 percent to 10 percent; and wireless will grow from 1 percent to 8 percent. These changes are not the result of pure cannibalization of the different pay providers but are part of a pie that is growing as fewer households receive free TV.

The Advertising Environment

Several factors drive advertising growth. The most important is the economy. Statistical analysis shows that, during the past 30 years, advertising has moved almost perfectly in line with nominal GDP. In fact, the R^2 is about 0.92. In individual years, however, advertising will tend to grow faster or slower than the economy for 5-year or 10-year swings, often as advertisers shift from using promotions, such as coupons, to brand identity advertising. For example, from 1976 to 1987, advertising grew faster than the economy; from 1988 to 1992, advertising grew slower than the economy.

During the recent period, promotional expenditures exploded. For example, Budweiser had the Bud Bowl promotion during the Super Bowl. With every case of Budweiser, consumers would get a coupon that could win a sweepstakes if they guessed the right score. More recently, the Bud Bowl has been de-emphasized. Now, Budweiser is doing brand identity advertising, such as the three frogs saying, "Bud-wise-er."

In 1994 and 1995, advertising grew faster than the economy. In 1995, total advertising grew about 7.7 percent while nominal GDP grew 5.1 percent. This growth followed a period of underperformance. In 1991, the worst year in advertising since 1961, advertising expenditures were down 1.6 percent. In 1992, while the economy grew at an annual rate of 5.2 percent, growth in advertising was only about 4 percent. This trend continued until the second half of 1993, when advertising finally grew faster than GDP.

The last factor driving growth in advertising expenditures is share shifts. Currently, the largest share shift is away from newspapers. Newspapers' share of local advertising has dropped from 53 percent to 48 percent in the past decade. As a share of total advertising in the past decade, newspapers declined from 27 percent to 22 percent. TV is down slightly from 21 percent to 20 percent. Radio has been stable at 7 percent and is gaining share locally.

Most of the gain, however, is being seen in cable, which has moved from 3 percent to 7 percent.

Sector Overviews

For each sector, this section discusses industry themes, growth trends, the leaders, the private market value activity (takeover activity), the regulatory environment, the key success criteria, and what to look for when valuing stocks.

Television

Currently, the biggest theme in the TV industry is the power shift from the networks to the TV stations. This change was sparked by the deal in which New World Communications Group shifted its affiliates (mostly CBS) to Fox, creating an affiliate war. Another factor was the launch of two more networks—Warner Brothers (WB) and United Paramount Network (UPN)—creating a game of musical chairs. Many U.S. markets have only four or five over-the-air TV stations. When only three or four networks existed, the game of musical chairs was not very exciting. With six networks, the game has become exciting. Local stations have shifted their affiliations, and what the networks will pay those stations has increased substantially. For example, a company such as LIN Television, which used to get $2 million a year from NBC to carry its programming, now gets $10 million a year from NBC. This increase in payments has dramatically changed the characteristics of the business.

The payments to local stations are free money and have no costs associated with them. This increase in network compensation has created a secular improvement in the stations' margins. The industry is also helped by the fact that programming costs are flat because programming is in oversupply. Programming accounts for about 40 percent of most TV stations' operating costs, and for most companies, this cost category is flat to declining.

TV gets about half of its revenue from local advertising and is gaining from the declining share in newspaper advertising. TV is also benefiting from a favorable regulatory environment. In 1994, the rate of total television advertising growth was 9.9 percent, compared with 8.2 percent for all advertising media. Total media advertising outgrew the nominal GDP of 6.2 percent. TV advertising was strong in the first half of 1995 but slowed down in the fourth quarter, partly because of the slowdown in underlying economic growth. TV advertising growth for 1995 as a whole was only about 4.4 percent, compared with 7.7 percent for total advertising. We believe TV advertising will have a good year in 1996 because of the Olympics in Atlanta and political advertising. Political advertising should exceed $500 million in 1996, compared with $350 million in 1994. As illustrated in **Figure 1**, the local TV station share of total advertising has been increasing slowly. National TV advertising, however, has declined. The decline stabilized from 1991 to 1994 and then resumed in 1995.

Figure 1. Television Stations: Share of Local and National Advertising

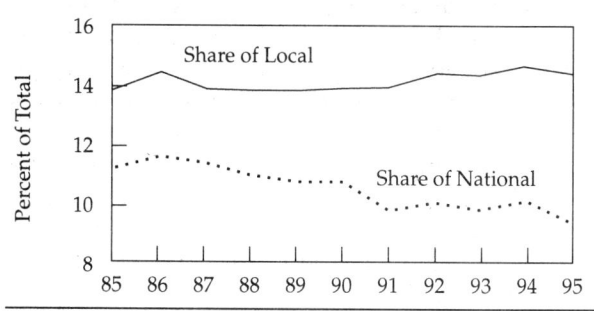

Source: Alex. Brown & Sons, based on data from McCann-Erickson.

Recently, audience shares, which had stabilized for the past few years, are falling off again. The networks doing the worst are CBS and ABC. The largest operators in the television sector, measured in national audience reach, are the station groups associated with the six networks: General Electric owns NBC; Westinghouse now owns CBS; Fox is owned by News Corp.; Tribune Company owns the station group for the WB network, which is owned by Time Warner; ABC is about to be owned by the Walt Disney Company; and Chris-Craft Industries is a station group for the UPN network.

Acquisition multiples are at an all-time high in the television sector. Outlet Communications was sold to NBC for 14 times cash flow, and an underperforming VHF station in West Palm Beach, Florida, sold for nearly 17 times cash flow. The rise in market value is in anticipation of looser ownership rules and is possible because senior lenders have been generous to broadcasters recently—in contrast to times when broadcasters have not been able to get money from senior lenders. From my perspective, I am concerned about companies taking too much money and leveraging themselves too much.

The regulatory environment is critical in analyzing media companies. Before the 1996 Telecommunications Act, a company could own only 12 television stations. In the new act, this limit is eliminated. The national audience cap (percentage of population a company's stations can cover) is limited to 25 percent, but the new act raises it to 35 percent. Westinghouse is at 34 percent. Tribune owns a minority stake in Quest, which brings it close to 35 percent also. Fox owns a minority stake in New World, which brings it over the 35 percent limit, if that ownership is attributed to it.

The Telecommunications Act does not specifically address the issue of whether a company may own two television stations in one market (TV duopoly), but the Federal Communications Commission (FCC) will rule on this question. Even though Congress has a deregulatory thrust and the chances of getting duopoly permission are good, it may not happen for a year or more. Television local marketing agreements (LMAs) are long-term leases with options to buy (pseudo-duopoly). About 40 currently exist in the country through a loophole. The new act appears to grandfather those already in effect, and the FCC will issue a ruling to determine whether LMAs will be allowed in the future. At the very least, the LMAs that have been put together by Clear Channel Communications, Sinclair Broadcast Group, and LIN Television, will probably survive.

With these new ownership rules, the industry should rapidly consolidate. Consolidation has several benefits. Television groups will be able to purchase programming less expensively. In general, a group buys programming for about 25 percent less than an individual station. Also, groups are able to share overhead. Larger companies typically have better access to capital both from the public markets, which have a bias toward size, and from the private markets. With TV duopolies, the LMAs that currently exist will tend to increase those stations' revenue shares and dramatically reduce programming costs. LMAs or duopolies typically have 25 percent lower costs than group owners.

In this consolidating environment, everyone is a winner. The networks will be able to own more stations. The majority of the profits are at the station level, so the networks want to own as many stations as possible. The medium-size groups will be able to merge together and achieve critical mass. TV duopolies have explosive growth potential. Television operators who do not want to be in the business or who do not want to compete should be able to exit at a decent price.

We use various criteria to value television companies. Tracking the past growth record and estimating how fast the company will grow in the future are important. Margins are critical, especially because acquisitions are important. Some operators are showing a 40 percent operating margin, and some are at 50 percent. If an operator that can consistently generate 50 percent cash flow margins buys a station with 40 percent, that acquisition will probably work.

Diversity is important. Companies should not be overly concentrated in one station or one region. Asset mix is critical. Is there vertical integration? Are there some programming assets? Like all media sectors, TV is management intensive, both in underlying growth and in use of cash flow. Finally, most investors like liquid stocks.

Radio Broadcasting

In the past few years, radio has been the fastest growing sector with regard to free cash flow. Running a radio station takes very little equipment. Most radio stations can be run in buildings the size of a conference room. This sector also benefits from consolidation, because the ownership rules changed in September 1992. The sector has had rapidly rising private market values since September 1992. The listenership has been stable at more than three hours per person a day during the week. Radio also benefits from having no technology threats; thus, capital expenditures can be low and predictable.

Radio has been gaining advertising share. As seen in **Table 2**, radio advertising grew faster than total advertising in 1993 and 1994. Local advertising grew faster than total station advertising in 1995. Radio should have another good growth year in 1996 at about 7.5 percent, both for stations and for the entire sector.

Table 2. Radio Advertising Recovery: Radio Advertising Growth

Category	1996[a]	1995	1994	1993
Total radio	7.6%	7.5%	11.3%	9.1%
Network	6.0	5.0	1.0	4.9
National spot	6.0	4.5	14.8	10.0
Local	8.0	8.3	11.2	9.2
Total station	7.6	7.6	11.8	9.3
Total advertising	7.2	7.7	8.2	5.3
Nominal GDP	5.0	5.1	6.2	5.4

[a]Estimated.

Source: Alex. Brown & Sons, based on data from the Radio Advertising Bureau and McCann-Erickson.

Over the past 10 years, newspapers have lost almost 5 share points in local advertising. All other local media benefit from that loss. About 80 percent of radio's advertising dollars are local, so share gain is critical to them. For television, about half the revenue is local, and for cable, local revenue is about 15 percent.

The 10 largest operators in radio include Westinghouse/CBS, Infinity Broadcasting, Evergreen Media Corporation, Disney, Chancellor, Cox Communications, Clear Channel, American Radio Systems, Jacor, and Viacom. Because the radio business exceeds $10 billion, even the largest operator—the new Westinghouse/CBS—has less than 5 percent of the total market. This sector is the most fragmented in the media industry. The top 10 operators account for only 25 percent of the entire radio business, and the top two account for less than 9 percent. These top 10 companies should be dramatically different as the ownership rules change.

As with television, radio acquisition multiples are at an all-time high. Multiples are in excess of 12 times for top-10-market radio groups. The deals have included Evergreen buying Pyramid, Chancellor buying Shamrock, and Infinity buying Alliance, all at multiples in the area of 12.7 times. This sector is benefiting from size. In the past, radio companies could not get that large because of the ownership rules. In 1992, the rules changed from limiting companies to 12 AM and 12 FM stations to 20 AMs and 20 FMs and allowing one company to own two FMs in the same market. In the case of radio duopoly, 1 + 1 = 3, because owning two FMs in a market could produce 50 percent higher profits cumulatively than could one FM. That fact has helped the results of the companies in this sector. Also, this sector is another in which senior lenders are being very open, which they were not in the past.

The relief is dramatic on the regulatory side. In addition to the 1992 relaxation of the rules governing number of stations, the new act erases the ownership limit on the number of stations, so a company can own an unlimited number of stations. For the first time, clusters are allowed, so in the top 10 markets, one company can own eight stations, five of which could be FMs. In the top 100 markets, a company can own six or seven stations, four of which can be FMs, which is practically like having no rules at all.

As a sector consolidates, it realizes several benefits from diversification and critical mass. In radio, clusters are more profitable than single stations in a market. A company can dominate a format—for example, own both the rock and classic rock stations. A company can have enhanced knowledge of a local market; for example, if the company has several stations in Atlanta, it gets to know all the advertisers in Atlanta and the pulse of the economy. The risk is also lower; for example, a market such as Boston, which used to have 20 competitors, is down to 6 competitors. Moreover, most of those competitors tend to be large, sophisticated companies that are all trying to expand their businesses. This sector has been hurt in the past by mom-and-pop operators that give advertising away for free and are willing to lose money because their wealth is elsewhere. Larger companies can share overhead and have greater access to financing.

Diversification is the most important factor to look for when valuing radio broadcasting stocks. We will pay a much higher multiple for diversified growth than for nondiversified growth. Individual stations can be volatile, and stations change formats. A company could have a format attack, no matter how well it is doing. Individual stations can get blind-sided occasionally. A big problem when a company could own only seven stations was that each station was typically a fairly large percentage of the company. In the 1980s, most companies derived more than half of their cash flow from two stations alone. Today, many broadcasters get less than one-quarter of their cash flow from their two largest stations. For example, if Infinity's number one station lost all its cash flow, the company's total cash flow would be down less than 10 percent.

Internal growth and acquisition growth are important. We look at station cash flow growth and the company's acquisition track record. Radio is a consolidating sector, so a company's ability to redeploy excess cash creatively is important. Audience share (strength) is another important measure. Finally, appropriate leverage is a factor. Given the unpredictability at individual stations, we want companies with large portfolios, but we want to be careful with leverage. With radio having virtually no capital requirements, if a company wants to be aggressive, it can go for a lot of leverage. In the late 1980s, several radio companies had 9 times debt leverage and many of them went bankrupt. We believe debt leverage should be much more moderate. Our litmus test is a ratio of debt to debt to earnings before interest, taxes, depreciation, and amortization (EBITDA) of about 6 times.

Cable Television

The cable sector has been under pressure during the past few years. New competitors have emerged: MMDS (microwave or wireless cable), telephone companies, private cable, and DBS. The FCC has been on a course of micromanagement. With the new act, however, that supervision will soften. Cable companies are looking to get into telephony. Some are involved with Sprint, an alliance creating both opportunity and uncertainty. Cable continues to be the only broadband pipe into the home, creating many potential opportunities. Two years ago, we were talking about the full-service network (FSN), interactivity, and pay-per-view. Currently, the talk is cable modems. With those opportunities, the industry's capital expenditures continue to be high, so it is important for companies to be large and have a lot of resources, which is why consolidation continues. In the past 10 years alone, the top

MSOs have gone from owning 45 percent of all cable subscribers to owning 74 percent.

Basic cable revenue is about 68 percent of total industry revenues. Revenue from premium channels has declined from 43 percent in 1985 to 20 percent in 1995. Miscellaneous revenue accounted for 5 percent in 1985 and has not grown in the past 10 years, but this activity offers a lot of opportunity in the future.

Growth has been solid but slow in the past five-year period compared with the previous five-year period. From 1990 to 1995, about 8 million subscribers were added, compared with 15 million subscribers added in the previous five-year period. In the five years just past, the average monthly bill increased a little more than $4.00 compared with an $8.00 increase in the previous five-year period. This decline was the result of the reregulation of this sector.

The 10 largest cable operators service about three-quarters of all subscribers. Tele-Communications Inc. (TCI) and Time Warner are the largest cable companies.

Unlike television and radio, acquisition multiples in cable have compressed because the regulatory environment has hurt cash flow growth. Also, the expectation was that capital expenditures should be dropping off, not ramping up. Thus, multiples have declined from a peak of almost 13 times in 1989 to slightly under 10 times in 1995.

Cable was reregulated in the 1992 Cable Act. The companies were forced into rate regulation and constraints on tiering. They also had to pay many television operators to carry their signals or be forced to put over-the-air channels on the cable system, a requirement that may have eliminated opportunities to carry a cable channel from which a company might have received some subscriber fees. The new act features staggered rate deregulation. In March 1999, many of the reregulatory rules will disappear and will move toward basic-only regulation, making packaging easier. The act allows cable companies to get into the telephone sector, but the telephone companies are also getting into the video sector. Having the RBOCs and cable companies competing head-to-head will trigger a relaxation in many of the regulations. Apparently, retransmission and must-carry requirements will stay around in the new act.

Among the several valuation criteria, size is important, especially in national and regional clusters. Clusters improve efficiency. Management should be aware of the competitive landscape; the key to operating a successful cable company is the ability to balance good core growth with making money in new areas. We like companies that have been upgrading their plant. Technological improvements such as fiber optics and increased channel capacity will give companies a competitive advantage in new endeavors and will give them more reliability and better-quality pictures. Customer service has been a problem in this industry, but the cable companies have made major strides in improving it. Cable was hurt when the companies did not know the regulatory rules of the game. If the rules are defined, most cable managements are probably nimble enough and have sufficient alternate revenue sources to do very well.

Wireless Cable

Wireless cable is a small but potentially lucrative niche in the expanding multichannel marketplace. The RBOCS have moved into this sector in the past year. Companies such as Bell Atlantic, NYNEX Corporation, and Pacific Telesis Group (PacTel) have made acquisitions in this sector, giving it the credibility it lacked earlier. A key issue for wireless cable is the move to digital signals. Because wireless has no wired plant, it can switch to digital faster than wired cable can. A wireless company can switch its transmitter from transmitting analog signals to digital signals and simply replace the analog box with digital boxes in the customers' homes. Wireless is still a small enough niche that replacing all those boxes is physically possible. Wired cable equipment is harder to replace because there is much more of it and the companies have to upgrade their wired plant. Potentially, wireless cable could provide more channels for less money than the wired cable operators and could maintain this advantage for some time. In fact, some observers believe that this is an interim technology that does have a competitive advantage for the short term.

One long-term uncertainty in this sector is that it is a broadcast medium, so it is not two-way, even though a telephone line can be used as a return loop. Near term, however, wireless has some advantages. Regulators have allowed wireless cable to get access to programming, and the sector was helped by some of the predatory pricing restraints against the cable companies. Wireless also has low-cost infrastructure per subscriber. This product does especially well where cable competition is very weak or nonexistent—for example, in areas too rural for cable to wire the homes. Where cable competition is not present, wireless can get 40 percent penetration. Against cable competition, 10 percent penetration is a more reasonable expectation.

Wireless has been growing rapidly. In 1995, the industry dramatically expanded the amount of line of sight (LOS) homes capable of receiving wireless cable signals. The finance community, including the public marketplace, has been willing to give this sector money, and it is also receiving money from the RBOCs.

Table 3 surprises many people. In many places, usually where cable competition is weak, wireless cable has fairly high penetration rates. Heartland Wireless Communications in Ada, Oklahoma, has penetration approaching 27 percent. This is a relatively rural area. The companies are also finding very low turnover, perhaps because people do not move around much in rural areas.

Table 3. Wireless Cable Industry: Top 15 Systems by LOS Penetration

Ticker Symbol	Location	Subscriber Penetration
Heartland	Ada, OK	26.8%
Private	Charlottesville, VA	25.0
American Telecasting	Yankton, SD	17.0
Heartland	Corpus Christi, TX	14.3
American Telecasting	Rapid City, SD	13.6
Heartland	Stillwater, OK	13.3
American Telecasting	Bend, OR	12.5
Private	Yakima, WA	11.6
American Telecasting	Colorado Springs, CO	11.4
Private	Ft. Pierce, FL	10.8
Pacific Telesis Group	Riverside, CA	10.8
Private	Boise, ID	10.2
American Telecasting	Windom, MN	10.2
People's Choice TV	Tucson, AZ	10.2
Private	Melbourne, FL	9.5

Sources: Company reports.

The private market value in wireless has been robust. Prices per line-of-sight (LOS) home have been about $100–$150 where LOS has high penetration, and the systems are actually EBITDA positive. They drop to $10–$30 per subscriber where the system is basically unbuilt. Interestingly, the RBOCs have migrated toward the bottom of the range because they are interested in the digital capabilities of wireless; thus, they have been unwilling to pay for analog subscribers. They are looking at the potential of wireless in a digital world.

The largest operators in this sector include American Telecasting, Heartland, CAI Wireless Systems (partially owned by Bell Atlantic and NYNEX), People's Choice TV, PacTel, Wireless One, and CS Wireless.

The regulatory environment is favorable in wireless. At one time, wireless had trouble getting CNN, and if a company did get it, the cable company would charge an exorbitant rate. The 1992 Cable Act forced the cable networks, which are owned by the cable MSOs, to give programming to wireless cable at a competitive price. That change was critical for the wireless companies. The FCC looks at wireless cable as new competition for cable, and it is trying to encourage new competition.

There are several success factors in this management-intensive niche. Companies need to balance their growth against their churn. Churn can be devastating in wireless because if someone cancels a wireless cable subscription, the company must collect the converter box and remove the antenna from the roof, which can be very costly. We like to see companies with 3 percent or less churn per month. Customer service is important. One of this sector's competitive advantages has been the ability to serve customers better than cable. Because this sector is an early-stage industry trying to increase its subscribers rapidly, marketing costs are important. Also, the companies need to look at who their competitors are and use different strategies against different competitors. We like companies that have former cable managers in their upper managements and thus know the competition.

As for valuation criteria, we tend to be selective because this sector is so management intensive. We like to focus on companies with a high growth rate in their analog system and a digital strategy with which we agree. If a manager knows the company is going to convert to digital, why try to expand the analog subscribers? In the end, the company will simply have to collect the analog boxes back. We like companies with weak competition, and topography is critical. A very hilly or wooded area will have fewer LOS homes. As with wired cable, clustering is effective. Having an RBOC partner is something we view positively. Because this sector is growing, companies must watch their financing. They can run out of money quickly, so they must manage their balance sheets prudently.

Conclusion

All of these media sectors are seeking critical mass, and deregulation creates the opportunity to achieve it. The consolidation occurring in most of these sectors creates the need for critical mass in order to be competitive. The desire for growth is the thrust for building critical mass.

Over the long term, these sectors will generally do very well because of the underlying health of the advertising market and the lucrative opportunities presented by technological innovations. Analysts must be cognizant of a company's underlying growth and how its management views excess cash flow. As an analyst, I find this industry very exciting to follow.

Question and Answer Session

Andrew W. Marcus, CFA

Question: Is DBS a good business? It has many new entrants who have made huge capital expenditures, but it has only about 10 percent of the overall television households. How will this sector shake out?

Marcus: It is a little too soon to tell. For homes that have no other choice, DBS is a needed product. It also tends to be a very good early-adaptor product for people with large TV sets who are price-insensitive buyers.

Historically, most consumers have either cable or nothing. Now, different products are available at different price points, and the selection will increase over time. DBS will probably be a high-end product. As cable and others ramp up their quality, DBS may lose some of its quality advantages and turn into more of a value product over time. What is important for DBS in the future is that consumers should not have to pay $700 up front as they do today and that the monthly fee should be reasonable. In the long term, there will be room for several different niches, and DBS will be one of them.

Question: With all of these new entrants to the broadcasting and cable television sector, how can margins hold up?

Marcus: We look at different aspects of profitability, such as the margins of the programmers, the margins of the television stations, and the margins of the people delivering the service. Over time, the conduit providers (delivering video into the home) will become more commoditylike as consumers have more conduits and choices; as a result, those margins should get compressed. In the past, the content providers—the companies that own the television shows—could sell that television show only to one of the big networks; now, they can start selling it to cable and in the future will be able to sell it to the RBOCs or DBS providers. In fact, if the show is a rerun, they can sell it over and over again. Over time, the content providers will see a margin appreciation.

Question: Many television and radio acquisitions have taken place. Could you define what you are talking about with multiples, EBITDA, broadcast cash flow, and so forth? What are those, and how do we look at them? When does some of this flurry of activity end? Are we not moving into some pretty heavy valuations?

Marcus: The multiples in our chart are the price to the broadcast cash flow multiple. Broadcast cash flow is defined as EBITDA before corporate expenses, and we are looking at it on a trailing 12-month basis. Multiples will be driven by growth, required rate of return, and cost of capital. Currently, the cost of capital is decreasing because the senior lenders are being more generous and because we are in a favorable interest rate environment. As the business becomes less risky and more diversified, people are willing to accept a lower required rate of return.

With regard to growth, we are seeing clusters growing faster than stand-alone stations. In general, growth is accelerating, thus driving multiples up. Current multiples in the top 10 markets are 12.7 times. That multiple is more than ample under certain scenarios. If an FM station in New York is being sold, in theory, someone can pay more if they already own one or two FM stations in New York. For television and radio, although we are at historic highs, these multiples can be sustained, especially in light of another round of deregulation, which should initiate aggressive consolidating activity. For the next three years or so, the industry will rapidly consolidate at very heady multiples, and then, on a normalized basis, it will move back down to a 10 or 11 multiple. For the next few years, multiples could rise as we get new ownership rules.

Question: What will the shift from analog to digital cost? What kind of capital expenditures are you currently projecting in the cable industry, and how do you see that competitive marketplace shaking out? Who has the advantage?

Marcus: The cost numbers differ. Switching to digital will be most costly for the RBOCs and less costly for the cable companies, because the cable companies already have a broadband network into the home. It will be least expensive for wireless cable. DBS is already on digital. Once the bird is in the sky, it sends digital signals to the home. We must also examine the cost of television stations switching to digital as we move to high-definition television (HDTV). These cost numbers are moving around because technology changes each year, making the cost less expensive. One of the most important costs is the digital converter box. The converter box will probably come out later this year for

The Media Industry

$300–$400, and this price should come down rapidly over time.

Question: When will MSOs ever show earnings or generate free cash?

Marcus: Some MSOs are generating free cash. This business tends not to be run for earnings. To be able to run your business without generating earnings is wonderful, because you do not have to pay taxes. Over time, however, you will eventually generate earnings. But the companies are free cash generators, and although some of them do not generate as much as we would hope, they will start being earnings generators. I am not sure they will ever pay dividends, but they should become earnings generators fairly soon.

Question: Could you be more specific as to what the duopoly limits will be? How many radio stations will a company be able to own in one market? For example, can you own five FM stations in the New York market?

Marcus: As a result of the new act, in markets with more than 44 stations (typically the top 10 markets), a company can own eight stations. Among those eight stations, five can be of one type of service (e.g., five FMs or five AMs). In markets with 30–44 stations (typically the top 50 markets), you can own seven stations, four FMs or AMs. In markets with 15–29 stations (typically the top 100 markets), you can own six stations, with four FMs. In markets with fewer than 15 stations, you are only allowed to own three FMs, with a maximum of five stations. Under these new rules, you could own five FMs and three AMs in New York.

Question: You did not talk a lot about newspapers, but if you look at the advertising shares, the "other" category has grown dramatically and newspapers have stayed relatively flat. What is in that "other" category, and what potential does it have? How do you see newspapers developing? Are they going to lose more share because of the consolidation of TV and radio or will some other revenue streams develop?

Marcus: The biggest portion of the "other" category is direct mail, which would be the promotion line. Direct mail has seen its share increase over the past few years. Also included are the yellow pages, which have been a steady grower, and magazines and outdoor advertising. Newspapers are losing share as their readership ages and declines. We expect the decline in newspapers to accelerate.

Question: There has been a lot of talk about spectrum auctions. Obviously, it is an issue facing the FCC. What is going to happen? Does this mean the end of free TV, or is this another way of taxing the development in the industry?

Marcus: The Dole provision to auction off the future HDTV spectrum would mean the end of free TV. Twenty-eight percent of homes today are getting television for free, and 20 percent of homes will likely get it for free five years from now. Many people in that 20 percent cannot afford to buy television, which is a reason for free television in this country. Television broadcasters contend that they are already paying money, because they are being forced to build HDTV capabilities, which will cost them a lot of money in equipment relative to their profits, especially for small market operators. To maintain the current free TV broadcasting system and to have a gradual transition to HDTV, you cannot auction off the spectrum.

Question: You indicated that advertising expenditures tend to be a function of GDP, but it seems to be outpacing GDP right now. When will that end? What will this pattern mean for some of those media companies and stocks?

Marcus: The promotion–advertising pendulum (in other words, the marketer's decision whether to use coupons or advertising), which will drive whether total advertising grows faster or slower than GDP, tends to swing slowly. Advertising grew faster than the economy for 11 years, then it grew slower than the economy for 5 years. Now we are in Year 2.5 or Year 3 of outperforming, and advertising could continue to outperform for quite a while. To determine the impact on specific companies, you need to look at individual media to see what is happening. Clearly, local newspapers, which still garner 48 percent of the total, are losing share. Other local media are likely to grow faster than the economy; and thus, the stocks have a good chance of outperforming.

Question: What are the prospects for some of the new TV networks? You mentioned that we have gone from three to six networks, but at the same time, we have seen the network share of viewers decline. Is it possible for these six to survive?

Marcus: Prevailing wisdom holds that it is unlikely that both WB and UPN can survive. In fact, there have been rumors that the two are considering merging. Although the UPN and WB network owners would like to merge, a merger is a problem at the station-group level because Tribune wants to be the station group and so does Chris-Craft. Only one of the two will survive over time, so it makes a lot more sense for them to merge. The one that will survive will be the one with the best shows. The reason networks tend to get more viewership share than niche networks is that the networks, by being broader, can spend more money on programming, which means they have a greater chance of producing a popular show. The concept of the network is to have a global or national program supplier that can do expensive programming and buy sports rights and then to have the individual stations or cable systems support that network.

Question: Do you see Internet access as a requirement to compete with a full package of services?

Marcus: We expect the Internet to become an advertising niche of more than $1 billion in the next decade. It should become another potential medium for a media plan, but not a necessary one.

Question: How do you think the growth of the Internet will affect the cable industry?

Marcus: It will be another competitor for advertising dollars. It could, however, help drive the success of ancillary cable services, if the cable medium works.

Question: If the DBS operators start giving their DBS units away for free (as cellular services have done), what kind of cable subscriber attrition do you foresee?

Marcus: Under that scenario, which is unlikely, DBS would severely hurt cable.

Question: What is the current language in the Telecommunications Act regarding foreign ownership of broadcast media? Are there specific rules for foreign duopoly?

Marcus: A non-U.S. company can own no more than 25 percent of a radio or TV license, with no restrictions on ownership of newspapers, TV networks, or cable systems.

Question: Under valuation criteria, you place some emphasis on diversification. Why is this important, given that portfolio managers could purchase more than one media stock and thus create the diversification?

Marcus: Any portfolio manager will tell you that the avoidance of picking losers is one of the keys to outperformance.

Question: Are radio programming costs significant? Is radio's untapped pricing power in ad rates? The ad rates seem pretty cheap.

Marcus: Radio's programming is composed of music, disc jockeys, and news, each of which is inexpensive. The most unpredictable cost is promotion. The key to revenue growth is audience ratings, which drive ad rates. As the industry consolidates and does a better job of competing against other media, we expect rates to rise.

Question: In radio, will consolidation keep providing value? Where will the shake-out end?

Marcus: We believe the consolidation will not end until the top 10 owners control 75 percent of the industry. The radio sector should evolve to 2–6 competitors per market, compared with the current 20 per market. This shift should be very healthy for the industry and accelerate its growth.

A Valuation Framework

Mario J. Gabelli, CFA
Chairman
Gabelli Funds, Inc.

Mayo T. Smith
Assistant Vice President
Gabelli & Company, Inc.

> Investors interested in media stocks face two challenges: understanding the myriad changes affecting the industry and knowing how to value the companies competing in such an environment. Trends toward global consumerism and global consolidation and advances in distribution technology will create new markets for some companies. For those who wish to capitalize on these opportunities, the key is to identify a catalyst that will cause the stock to approach its intrinsic value and to wait for the market to realize that value.

The rapidly changing structure of the media industry and the companies within it makes these stocks particularly difficult to value. Doing so requires experience with and a thorough understanding of the industry. In "The Media Industry: A Look Ahead," Mayo T. Smith reviews important future investment themes and places these in the context of the history of the industry. Mario Gabelli then explains Gabelli Funds' approach to valuation techniques in "The Media Industry: A Valuation Approach." He calls upon the knowledge he gained from being an owner, analyst, and officer of companies in the media industry. This experience provides unique insights into the art of valuation for this sector.

The Media Industry: A Look Ahead

Several investment themes will dominate the market in the future. Many of these themes should benefit the American economy and the stock market. With the Dow Jones Industrial Average above 5000, the ability to identify the correct themes in advance will be particularly important for capital preservation and wealth generation.

Global Consumerism

Perhaps the biggest opportunity for U.S. companies is global expansion. Ninety-five percent of the world's population is outside the United States. Three billion people are in the Pacific Rim, China, and India, where GDPs are growing at double-digit rates. This growth is a boon for U.S. goods and services. During the past four years, in India alone, the number of satellite dishes in use has increased from 400,000 to more than 10 million. Think of what that implies for U.S. content producers such as Time Warner and Viacom.

Strategic Global Consolidation

Another important theme is global consolidation. The first round was in the 1960s with conglomerates such as ITT and Gulf & Western. In the 1980s, financial intermediaries such as Drexel Burnham & Lambert dominated the leveraged buyout scene. Then came General Electric's attempt to take over Kemper Corporation in 1994, which we felt would have tremendous significance—and it did. Since then, we have witnessed the third round of takeovers.

Viacom's acquisition of Paramount in 1993 was only the beginning of the media mating game. This activity intensified in 1995 with Disney/Cap Cities, Westinghouse/CBS, and Time Warner/Turner Broadcasting System. There is almost a deal a day at this point. Creativity and content companies need to ensure distribution of their products, and distribution companies need to guarantee a supply of programming. Everyone is looking for a suitable partner. The party will not be over for some time, and it is hard to predict who will ultimately go home together.

The proposed merger between Time Warner and Turner Broadcasting offers investors a global media entity with outstanding long-term growth potential: an unrivaled film library to feed into expanding distribution systems in the United States and abroad. The marriage involves the most consistently profitable film entertainment producer and market-share leader in recorded music with the most creative cable network package in the world—a combined company with the financial muscle to take its products to the far corners of the globe.

What U.S. products travel well? In addition to Coca-Cola and blue jeans, the answer is cartoons, sports, movies, and music. So, each of the mergers that have been discussed has opportunities. The question is: How do the opportunities translate into profits for our clients? Deals are a way to unlock the value of a business. Deals create an exit strategy and help with our ability to harvest profits.

Communication of Ideas

One of the most dramatic themes for the future is the communication of ideas. The technological revolution in communications is transforming the economic and social dynamics of our universe. Instant communications and the free flow of information worldwide are changing how we live, work, learn, and play.

The revolution in communications is sweeping through human society in a way that changes everything everywhere. It is bringing people, places, and ideas together in new ways and changing the way we think.

Changes in the ways ideas are communicated, from Gutenberg to Gates, have had a profound effect on society. Consider the following timeline:
- In 1455, Johannes Gutenberg printed the first book for mass distribution—the Bible. Prior to that, everything was laboriously written by hand. This method of casting type and printing was so successful that its fundamental principles were not improved until well into the 19th century.
- The first electronic language was the telegraph. In 1831, Samuel Morse devised the telegraph system and sent the first message, "What hath God wrought," from Baltimore to Washington, D.C. The management of the gigantic, 19th century British Empire was only possible thanks to the telegraph.
- In 1876, Alexander Graham Bell transmitted the first telephone message, "Watson, come here. I need you." A medieval king would have needed legions of horsemen riding for months to deliver one-thousandth the number of messages we can transmit today in a few moments to the ends of the earth by phone or fax.
- In 1926, Charles Jenkins transmitted the first images via television. The first telecasts regularly scheduled for the public began in London in 1936. One million receivers were in use in America in 1949, 10 million by 1951, and more than 100 million by 1975.
- Because of the computer revolution, each of us in the modern world has more machine power available at our fingertips than any Roman emperor. The wealthiest man in the United States today is William Henry Gates III, the co-founder of Microsoft, which is responsible for the most popular personal computer operating system (the software that runs the machines).

The Future

How do we reap the benefits of this new technology? What will the 21st century look like? Let's talk about new outlets first. Wireless cable, direct broadcast satellite (DBS) service, and video dial tone will all increase the demand for entertainment programming. In addition, more than 25 million homes have personal computers and more than 5 million of them subscribe to online services. CD-ROM is already part of the Hollywood vocabulary.

Publishers, film makers, and music recording companies are all working on new products specifically for the booming home computer market. Consumers want to manipulate video, text, and music. A portion of our clients' portfolios will be invested in copyright and creativity for the interactive couch potato. These stocks range from music companies to newspaper companies, and they are available globally. The new generation of couch potatoes wants to create its own shows, opening up an entirely new market for the content creators. With an increased number of distribution channels and an expanding world economy, the opportunities for the content creators are as big as their imaginations.

For all of these companies, the future offers new outlets and new markets. MTV is now in more homes outside the United States than in the United States. It is the Coca-Cola of content creators.

New outlets, new products, and new markets translate into profits for our clients. Companies see rising economic activity and profits. When a gap develops between the public market price of a stock and the private market value of the business, something will happen to fill that gap. Deals will refocus attention on the franchise values of cable, communications, and entertainment, which we believe are significantly higher than current stock prices.

The Media Industry: A Valuation Approach

The world of entertainment has changed. When I started in the business 30 years ago, for example, a movie such as *Cleopatra* would generate 25 cents in overseas revenues for every dollar generated domestically. These days, a movie such as *Waterworld* will generate twice as much revenue overseas as it does in the domestic market. This type of change is common throughout the media industry, and we have had to adapt our analytic approach to reflect this new reality.

Research Methodology

In the early 1970s, I visited car companies in Japan as a sell-side analyst. I had no interest in recommending Japanese stocks. I wanted to understand the dynamics: what these car companies were doing and how they would affect the demand, cost structure, and pricing structure of the U.S. automobile industry. We changed that approach about eight years ago and now look at companies that have competence within our area of expertise. Our analysts are expected to know how Compania de Telecomunicaciones de Chile S.A. and Telefonica de España S.A. are structured, what their ownerships are, and what their valuations are.

Each analyst is expected to develop an operational understanding of his or her industry. They hone this expertise by continually talking to competitors, suppliers, and customers. In addition, the analysts develop and maintain government and trade sources to derive an overall understanding of their industries.

Valuation Process

We approach security analysis as fundamentalists, investing primarily in the equities of cash-generating franchise companies that are selling in the public market at a significant discount to our fundamental appraisal of their intrinsic value. Our approach to fundamental research focuses on three aspects: free cash flow (earnings before interest, taxes, depreciation, and amortization—EBITDA) minus the capital expenditures necessary to grow the business; earnings per share (EPS) trends; and private market value (PMV), which encompasses on- and off-balance-sheet assets and liabilities.

All of our analysts project earnings per share for five years. We look at EPS because it is the standard with which everyone is comfortable. What is the EPS for Westinghouse in the year 2000 pro forma for the leveraged buyout it did of CBS? What is the value of the enterprise if Seagram wants to own it? What is the cash flow? The nonquantifiable ingredient is very important.

Our valuations and methodologies are fairly straightforward. We look at the public price relative to the underlying values, which are driven by EBITDAs and the capital expenditures required to maintain those EBITDAs. We look at these businesses more through the eyes of a Kohlberg Kravis Roberts (KKR) than we do through the eyes of a corporate buyer. A corporate buyer could drop the back office and the overhead and get substantial synergistic benefits. The benefit to the KKRs of the world is that they can energize lazy assets. So, we view valuations in the private market.

Using PMV investing methodology as a benchmark for public market investing is very difficult. Netscape Communications' per share price went from $28 to $180 in six months, a hard standard to use. The standards were a little easier for America Online, but PMV investing changes. In 1968, a company could go out and raise 10 cents on the dollar and borrow 90 cents. The equity costs were 35 percent, and the subordinated debt was 15–18 percent. This situation allowed for a different multiple of EBITDA to be paid than we find in today's markets.

We factor in several variables such as the PMV in 1996 and in the year 2000—when we want to sell. When Turner Broadcasting spent $750 million bidding in the recent auctions for cellular licenses, what was it paying for and why? What internal rates of return were used? When MCA buys a record company's contract, what is it thinking about doing, how does it leverage the company up, and what kind of returns is it getting globally? What are the changes that would affect our valuations and the growth rates? EBITDAs grow because of top-line synergistic benefits and the like.

Company Management

Not only do we need for the numbers to look good, we also want to have strong management. We continually visit hundreds of companies' managements and integrate their input with our knowledge base. Our goal is to understand management's motivations and expectations. Given our long-term approach, we want to know who our partners are and whether they are working to enhance shareholder value. This process, coupled with our financial analysis, helps us select the most attractive investment candidates for our clients.

Industry-Specific Issues

Every industry has specific issues and concerns that we have to review and understand. In the cable and television sectors, we have to understand the regulatory entities, what GDP is doing, and what is happening to personal consumption expenditures. We break down the advertising dollar into its various components. We talk to such companies as Procter & Gamble (P&G) to determine how they plan to spend advertising dollars and how they buy advertising in Europe or China. We try to understand how the U.S. advertising infrastructure follows the P&Gs globally: Around the world, as Coca-Cola goes, so do the advertiser-supported media. How do we leverage that up? Who is late in the game, and who is early?

When reviewing telephone companies, we look at the macro and micro factors that are of concern for any valuation. What will the economy be like? What will inflation be like? How regulated is the industry? How flexible is the pricing? Where is the demand coming from?

The regional Bell operating companies (RBOCs) are 11 years old. They are huge and ready to do a lot of deals. NYNEX wants to own Southern New England Telephone. Ameritech Corporation wants to own Cincinnati Bell. If Bell Atlantic merges with NYNEX, what does that mean for long distance? Some day, we may have more personal computers out there than television sets. What will happen to television levels, ratings, and share because everyone is on the Internet? What does that do to demographics? How does P&G get to the advertising? These other forms of entertainment fragment viewing. What does that mean for stock valuations? Those are some of the questions we address using our approach.

The Telecommunications Act of 1996 will be a major catalyst that will provide a lot of values through deals. What is global multimedia? Is it entertainment; telephone; cable, wired, or wireless; content; or distribution? The relevant question is whether the stock will provide a better risk-adjusted return over the next 10 years than the average stock has provided over the past 60 years. How do we value such stocks?

The Catalyst

After we have done the fundamental analysis of a company and put a valuation on it, then we look at the price of the stock relative to the band of private market values. If shares are trading above or below our valuation, we have an opportunity.

Identification of an undervalued situation does not necessarily guarantee a rewarding investment. The next step is to try to identify a catalyst that will cause the valuation in the market to approach our determination of the share's intrinsic value. The primary catalysts in the media industry are changes in the regulatory environment and merger and acquisition activity.

Long-Term Investing

The purchase of Manhattan Island in 1624 for $24 or $27 worth of trinkets is usually considered a terrific investment. Today, it is worth about $3 trillion to $4 trillion. That is only a 6 percent compounded return for a 380-year holding period. If you are long-term investors, that is the way to think about such matters, and that is what we do. We are postage stamp collectors. We are patient investors and are willing to wait for the market to recognize the value that we perceive.

Question and Answer Session

Mario J. Gabelli, CFA
Mayo T. Smith

Question: Which sectors will be the big winners from the Telecommunications Act?

Gabelli: The telephone sector is already seeing part of the effect with Pacific Telesis Group (PacTel) spinning off AirTouch Communications. You are seeing it with U S West tracking media group operations through the new U S West Media Group. You will see NYNEX and Bell Atlantic figure out something similar.

A concern for the smaller telephone companies is the risk of universal service, but we believe that the small telephone companies are good investments.

Question: Are you concerned that multiples for private deals are at an all-time high?

Gabelli: They may have been this high back in 1968, 1987, or 1988. There is some economic risk, but there are synergies that can drive the transactions. The cost of capital at these levels is justified if I can have a 6 percent revenue growth and a 3 percent inflation environment. Private market deals at 15 times EBITDA are stretching. There is no margin of safety.

The place to put money currently is in small telephone company distribution, whether it is wired or wireless. Some companies in the public market are selling at 6 or 7 times EBITDA. There are ways to make money in the markets, given that these companies are trading at valuations significantly below their private market values.

Question: What signals do you look for in exiting a stock? Will you sell a stock with a strong management team and strong growth but very high valuation?

Gabelli: In the case of Berkshire Hathaway, for the past 15 years, there was always a time to sell it. We tend to have a business dynamic. We will sell some stocks when they get too high in a specific portfolio. Basically, if we like a business, we will stay with it for a while. We have our own set of internal dynamics as to how we deal with stock as opposed to how we look at an industry. Right now, we avoid industries such as long distance, the major companies, and the marginal companies.

Question: What is the best pure play for digitalization or the best way to play it, such as digital video, high-definition television, or digital cable?

Gabelli: The best way to play digital television is through the vendors to cable, not through equipment manufacturers. If I am BET, Family Entertainment, or Liberty Media, I will have more channels for my product, so I can leverage an existing program, create more programming at a low cost, and have relationships with my vendors and distributors that make sense.

Question: Of public and private market values, which is right?

Gabelli: They are both right over time. I tend to be in the camp of those who say, "If I can buy 100 shares of stock at 16 or buy the whole company at 25, which will make me better off?" I like to know what a business is worth. Eventually management will do something if there is a large discrepancy between the private market value and the share's price in the public markets.

Interpreting the Industry Numbers

Lawrence J. Haverty, Jr., CFA
Senior Vice President
State Street Research and Management Company

> Enterprise value analysis is a useful methodology for analyzing the media industry. It has the strong economic grounding that is required to understand such a complex industry. It does, however, have some limitations that analysts should take into account when using it. These include the failure to take interest rates, and their market effects, into account; the need to adjust for sociological factors; and the requirement for accurate forecasts.

This presentation presents an analytical framework for a better methodology for understanding the industry from an investment standpoint. This methodology is called enterprise value analysis (EVA). The follies of using conventional analysis are examined by following the odyssey of a hypothetical "Film Company A." Although the numbers might be hypothetical, Film Company A's situation is often repeated in real life. The presentation also provides some definitions and conventions to help investment managers understand what people in this industry are talking about.

The Odyssey of Film Company A

In our world of computers, things are designed to happen fast. A firm's business does not accelerate linearly, but when it accelerates, it does so rapidly. The revenue and expense numbers for Company A are presented in **Table 1**. Film Company A's sales are shown to accelerate from $92 million in Year 1 to $602 million in Year 5. Its net income cycles from $14 million in Year 1 to $24 million in Year 4. So, although Company A had accelerating sales and should have had accelerating net income, it did not. So now, this story is kind of a mystery novel.

The first clue as to why earnings growth has not kept up with sales growth is that Film Company A is borrowing money. Interest expense, shown in Column 3 of Table 1, goes up exponentially, especially in Year 5. This signals that the company is using more cash than it is generating. The next clue is film inventories (Column 4). Once the company makes films and music, they go into inventory. It spends a certain amount of money (say $100 million) to produce a film, which then sits in inventory. Most inventories do not get better with age. Sales in Year 1 through Year 4 are up by three times, and film inventories are up by almost 20 times. Maybe this company has not been writing off its inventories. These are warning signs. In Year 5, all of this comes home to roost. The inventories are written down from $513 million to $258 million. Instead of accelerating net income, the company has a net loss of $228 million. We had a cash model on the real company that is represented here by Film Company A for every quarter of its existence. It never generated cash and the net income it generated was pure, unadulterated myth.

Definitions

Investing in firms like Film Company A is risky. Each year, new analysts think film companies are the greatest investments, but big losses have occurred in this industry. How can analysts prevent this disaster from happening? One way is to understand the business better. The following are some terms and conventions the industry uses:

■ *Broadcast cash flow.* This concept is earnings before interest, taxes, depreciation, and amortization (EBITDA) of program rights ex barter, plus noncash corporate compensation, plus corporate expense, minus cash payments for production. For television stations, this amount is a very good measure of the cash the station generates. Of course, investors are not buying the station, they are buying stocks, so corporate overhead is always

Table 1. The Odyssey of Film Company A
(millions of dollars)

Year	Sales	Interest	Film Inventories	Net Income
1	$ 92	$ 2	$ 25	$ 14
2	165	8	200	36
3	152	12	350	14
4	269	14	513	24
5	602	48	258	–228

Source: State Street Research and Management Company.

between the shareholder and the broadcast cash flow. If some of these guys are spending too much of the corporate overhead on lunch, there may not be any left for the shareholders, so watch out when using broadcast cash flow.

■ *Syndication*. If, say, Warner Bros. produces a television show, it will license the show to a network such as NBC. After the show finishes running on the network, the film company hopes to syndicate it and sell it to several hundred stations throughout the country. Sumner Redstone mentioned that Viacom expects to make $3 million per episode from the syndication of *Frasier*, a sitcom Paramount produces.[1] The margins on syndication are somewhere between 50 and 60 percent, so if 50 episodes of *Frasier* go into syndication, that is $150 million, pretax, for Viacom. Syndication is an excellent type of cash flow.

■ *Back end*. The back end is what happens in syndication. In television production, two things are important. One is the front end, such as licensing *Frasier* to NBC, and that probably does not cover the cost of production. The back end (syndication) is where all the profits are.

■ *Hidden assets*. If you go to a Time Warner presentation, you will be shown a chart with $6 billion of hidden assets. If you believe this, I have a bridge for you to buy. Many firms in this industry have hidden assets. We developed a convention of what was and was not a hidden asset. Something in production that is losing money, such as *Entertainment Tonight*, is not a hidden asset. In the managements' minds, it may be worth $400 million, but that is in the future growth of the company. It is the normal cost of doing business. If you are in the publication business, you have to spend money on new material. In contrast, Time Warner owns 22 percent of Turner Broadcasting System. Turner Broadcasting does not contribute to Time Warner's cash flow on a consolidated basis. It is off the balance sheet. It is something that can be precisely valued and is a hidden asset. We believe Time Warner has significant hidden assets, but we differ with what management believes the value of those assets is.

■ *EBITD*. This number is earnings before interest, taxes, and depreciation. It excludes corporate overhead (we already deducted corporate overhead before we got to EBITD). Time Warner will give an analyst the EBITD numbers of the divisions, but the analyst has to deduct the actual corporate overhead. Sometimes the operating earnings figures that these companies provide are not the numbers with which an analyst wants to work. Analysts want to work with EBITD.

■ *Gross participation and net participation*. The gross participation in a movie is a fraction of the film off the top. The net participation in a movie is what is left after all the studio overhead is deducted. There are more forms of studio overhead than there are stars in the sky, so there is never a net participation. If the company is giving people net participations, give the managers a star because they are bright. If the company is giving out gross participations on its films, watch out, because there may be nothing left for the shareholders.

■ *Distribution fee and license fee*. The distribution fee applies to the theater business. It is what the theater owner and the distribution company (e.g., Warner Bros.) take for distributing the movie. The film producer does not get 100 percent of the box office. Most of the time, the producer gets about 50 percent of the box office. Producers who use someone else to distribute a film get a lot less than 50 percent. The barrier to entry in this business is distribution. Distribution is a critical asset, which should not be underestimated. The real strength of Time Warner's film business is in its distribution.

■ *Returns*. Returns will come up in the next few weeks. In the music business, companies sell the music to the stores, but the stores have the right to return the music if it does not sell. The current environment in the retailing of music is abysmal. There are too many stores, and the product is not selling. In the latter half of 1996, someone in the music business will have a return problem. The problem will be analogous to that for Film Company A: Much of the earnings figure that was released was not actual earnings, because the product sat on the shelves.

■ *Film accounting*. When investing in a company in the film business, be very careful. Film accounting is very tricky. The companies incur the costs for the film now, but how they amortize the costs is up to them. Most big companies are very conservative and do not play accounting games. The smaller companies generally do play accounting games. If a film company is reporting earnings, those

---
[1] See Mr. Redstone's presentation, pp. 1–11

earnings may have nothing to do with cash. Be aware of how companies amortize their costs, whether they are in marketing or production. The revenues from a film can come in over a 3-, 5-, or even 10-year period, but all the costs are generally incurred in the year the film was produced.

■ *Syndication economics.* The television business is very bifurcated. Most comedy shows produced on the air are not very profitable. Shows such as *ER*, *Frasier*, or *Friends* are unmitigated bonanzas because they go into syndication and very few costs are left to go into the income statement. That revenue is genuine cash. When researching a big film company, ask the management about the syndication backlog. When are the programs that have been produced coming into syndication? When is the company likely to have syndication-related earnings? Syndication earnings are very lumpy: They come in one or two quarters.

Analytic Methodologies

Successful media investors must understand what they are doing and why they are investing in these companies. The common denominator is to make money. When investors own a stock, they own a business. They choose to own a business because it will grow and generate cash. Increasing barriers to entry may make the stream of cash more valuable. Therefore, investors would like either to purchase that business or to sell it at a fair price. The problem is now to value the stock and forecast its future.

The Conventional Approach

In this industry, achieving that goal is relatively complex. That complexity is an advantage for people who understand it, because the people who buy stock in this industry and sell it among themselves are in an exclusive club. The people who are not in it do not understand the language and get their brains beat in. They sell stock to us when they should buy and vice versa.

The problems with using conventional analysis in this industry are twofold. First, the companies are complex. For the Walt Disney Company, for example, which was one of the simpler companies before the Capital Cities/ABC deal, one analyst had 20 different earnings models for the television and film part of the company alone; those businesses did not include the theme parks and the consumer products. Second, conventional accounting does not work for entertainment companies. It does not help you get the right answer.

Enterprise Value Analysis

Equity value is defined as the market value of equity, less cash and hidden assets, and plus debt. **Table 2** illustrates a valuation analysis for 26 companies. The basic relationship is:

EBITD = Trailing four quarters EBIT + D + A.

We are not making any forecasts about EBITD. What is in the table is historical and reported. Instead, we estimate the value multiple, which is the ratio of the enterprise value to trailing EBITD:

Value multiple = Enterprise value/Trailing EBITD.

The value multiple has strong economic rationality. The value multiple inverted is essentially the pretax cash flow return on assets of the corporation. If British Sky Broadcasting Group (BSkyB) has an enterprise value to EBITD of 17.7, the inverse is 6 percent. If investors buy BSkyB at the price of $3, they are buying an asset that is returning 6 percent. They better hope that the company's cash flow grows rapidly, because 6 percent is low for a cash flow return. The Kroger Company is at a 7 multiple, which represents a 15 percent cash flow return. That is a good return if the investor can borrow at 8 percent and if Kroger's cash flow grows.

We use the three-year EBITD growth rate as a forecast of business operations. Any business does two things: It operates itself, and it finances itself. Try to segregate how much the operations will contribute from how the financial shenanigans will contribute. We look for a three-year EBITD growth rate in this industry because of the lumpy nature of the cash flows. Having a *Forrest Gump* helps Viacom's cash flow tremendously, but a *Forrest Gump* will not come around the corner every week. What analysts need to know is how fast that particular business will grow for three years. Most of the companies are happy to share their three-year cash flow forecasts, which represent their assessment of the operating factors.

The Importance of Free Cash Flow

The best businesses are those that generate the most cash. Businesses in this industry have very different cash-generating characteristics. For example, radio stations involve virtually no capital. Almost all of the cash flow that, say, Infinity Broadcasting generates is free. On the other hand, the cable industry will probably never have any free cash flow (FCF). You must adjust and compare Infinity Broadcasting or a television station with a cable operation.

In the "FCF adds" column in Table 2, we look for companies with low or no cash reinvestment. Two businesses that are terrific in this respect are radio and television stations and casinos. Slot machines entail no inventory or receivables; they generate cash.

Table 2. Valuation Analysis

Company	Price 7/27/95	Shares Outstanding[a]	Equity Value[a]	Hidden Assets[a]	Net Debt[a]	Enterprise Value[a]	Trailing EBITD[a]	Enterprise Value/EBITD	Estimated EBITD Growth	FCF Adds	Total Growth
BSY[b]	$ 3	1,715	$ 5,145	$ —	$ 900	$ 6,045	$ 341	17.7	40%	0%	40%
CBS	76	62	4,681	—	283	4,964	439	11.3	8	2	10
CCB	97	154	14,880	400	-837	13,643	1,485	9.2	12	4	16
CIR	31	86	2,634	—	581	3,215	332	9.7	20	0	20
CMCSA	21	240	4,950	700	5,694	9,944	644	15.4	25	0	25
DIS	57	532	30,457	1,100	1,213	30,570	2,764	11.1	18	2	20
GET	26	93	2,418	—	-15	2,403	159	15.1	22	0	22
GRTV10[c]	62	309	19,158	3,000	5,937	22,095	861	25.7	30	0	30
GTK	30	43	1,290	—	329	1,619	217	7.5	13	2	15
HET	27	103	2,807	—	455	3,262	371	8.8	25	0	25
HLT	72	49	3,516	—	867	4,383	427	10.3	15	0	15
HSN	9	91	796	—	-6	790	20	39.5	30	0	30
INFTA	34	45	1,519	300	524	1,743	129	13.5	22	4	26
KR	32	126	4,001	—	3,639	7,640	1,057	7.2	8	3	11
LIZ	23	75	1,734	—	-329	1,405	186	7.6	10	3	13
MAT	29	227	6,470	—	574	7,044	669	10.5	13	2	15
MGG	25	48	1,194	—	452	1,646	150	11.0	10	6	16
MIR	31	96	2,928	—	299	3,227	327	9.9	22	0	22
NWS[d]	8	2,750	22,000	8,500	6,633	20,133	1,872	10.8	12	3	15
PRH	25	52	1,281	—	188	1,469	129	11.4	25	0	25
PRMA	20	31	624	—	155	779	69	11.3	25	2	27
TBS.A	21	282	5,816	—	2,485	8,301	504	16.5	20	2	22
TCOMA	25	710	17,661	6,000	11,700	23,361	1,862	12.5	18	2	20
TWX	43	381	16,193	3,000	14,200	27,393	2,439	11.2	15	2	17
VIA	50	387	19,495	1,600	10,200	28,095	3,463	11.4	20	0	20
WAC	22	42	935	—	422	1,357	124	10.9	16	4	20

Key:
BSY	British Sky Broadcasting Group	
CBS	CBS Inc.	
CCB	Capital Cities/ABC	
CIR	Circus Circus Enterprises	
CMCSA	Comcast Corporation	
DIS	Walt Disney Company	
GET	Gaylord Entertainment Company	
GRTV10	Grupo Televisa	
GTK	Gtech Holdings Corporation	
HET	Hannah's Entertainment	
HLT	Hilton Hotels Corporation	
HSN	Home Shopping Network	
INFTA	Infinity Broadcasting	
KR	The Kroger Company	
LIZ	Liz Claiborne	
MAT	Mattel	
MGG	MGM Grand, Inc.	
MIR	Mirage Resorts, Inc.	
NWS	News Corp.	
PRH	Promus Hotel Corporation	
PRMA	Primadonna Resorts	
TBS.A	Turner Broadcasting System	
TCOMA	Tele-Communications Inc. (TCI)	
TWX	Time Warner	
VIA	Viacom	
WAC	The Warnaco Group	

[a] Amounts are in millions.
[b] Price is in British pounds.
[c] Price is in Mexican pesos.
[d] Price is in Australian dollars.

Source: State Street Research and Management Company.

Next, we need a methodology to deal with tax rates. If a company is paying a low real tax rate (we are interested more in the real tax rate than the book tax rate) but the taxes are going to go up, some of the cash flows are going to be used to pay taxes. Similarly, when companies own hidden assets that we think will grow in value, we need to account for that effect. For example, one of the reasons News Corp. stock exploded was that the hidden asset (ownership of BSkyB) was generating large amounts of cash flow and subscriber growth. We consistently escalated our value of BSkyB to News Corp. shareholders as a hidden asset, so that the stock became more attractive as it went up.

FCF can also be used to reduce interest costs. When Cap Cities was a public company, it was a tremendous FCF generator. Its interest expense went down every year. We estimated that the cash-generating nature of that business added 4 percent to its business cash flow growth (EBITD). Most of these companies are more or less cash neutral, if they are not making acquisitions.

Now that we have all these numbers, we use the measures in **Table 3** as a ranking mechanism.

We rank the companies by three variables: by the ratio of total growth to the enterprise value multiple, by EBITD growth, and by total growth. The companies at the top are generally the ones we want to buy, and the companies at the bottom are the ones we want to sell..

Benefits and Pitfalls

Among the pitfalls of the EVA method is the fact that it is independent of interest rates. It is a two-dimensional matrix. The stock market does react to interest rates, however. If an investor thinks rates are going to decline, that investor probably wants to pay higher EV multiples. If the cost of capital at the margin is 5 percent, you could probably afford to pay 11 times for a cable company. If the cost of capital is 12 percent and you pay 11 times, you will be out of business. These rankings are not determined in a vacuum. These companies are much less attractive in an environment in which interest rates are rising.

A second pitfall is that sociology establishes the value ratio range. At the top of the list is Harrah's Entertainment, Primadonna Resorts, Mirage

Table 3. Ranking Analysis

By Growth/Value Multiple		By EBITD Growth		By Total Growth	
HET	2.84	BSY	40%	BSY	40%
PRMA	2.39	GRTV10	30	GRTV10	30
BSY	2.26	HSN	30	HSN	30
MIR	2.23	CMCSA	25	PRMA	27
PRH	2.20	HET	25	INFTA	26
CIR	2.07	PRH	25	CMCSA	25
GTK	2.01	PRMA	25	HET	25
INFTA	1.92	GET	22	PRH	25
WAC	1.83	INFTA	22	GET	22
DIS	1.81	MIR	22	MIR	22
VIA	1.75	CIR	20	TBS.A	22
CCB	1.74	TBS.A	20	CIR	20
LIZ	1.72	VIA	20	DIS	20
CMCSA	1.62	DIS	18	TCOMA	20
TCOMA	1.59	TCOMA	18	VIA	20
KR	1.52	WAC	16	WAC	20
TWX	1.51	HLT	15	TWX	17
HLT	1.46	TWX	15	CCB	16
MAT	1.46	GTK	13	MAT	16
GET	1.46	MGG	13	GTK	15
MGG	1.42	CCB	12	HLT	15
NWS	1.39	NWS	12	MGG	15
TBS.A	1.34	LIZ	10	NWS	15
GRTV10	1.17	MAT	10	LIZ	13
CBS	0.88	CBS	8	KR	11
HSN	0.76	KR	8	CBS	10

Note: See Table 2 for key to stock symbols.
Source: State Street Research and Management Company.

Resorts, and Circus Circus Enterprises. Many people do not like to be involved with the casino industry, but it offers a lot of growth for a very reasonable price. Similarly, a company like Disney with a very clean image sells at 1.81. The real challenge in this ranking process is finding a company for which the value ratio is subject to change. Two companies that come to mind have been tremendous stocks for us. Mirage was regarded as a very marginal operator and is now regarded as the top casino operator. The value ratio in that company has improved by about 75 basis points. A company that meets the cash flow forecast and improves its value ratio by 75 bps will provide a 100 percent return in a very brief period. The second example is Infinity Broadcasting, which is currently trading at a cash flow multiple of 20. In July, Infinity traded at a 13.5 cash flow multiple. Of course, the reverse is also true. Investors lose money when the value range contracts. The value range in cable has been contracting for reasons of regulation and potential competition. Investors have to be careful about the range and watch what is happening. A change in a company's value ratio almost always has a good explanation. The market is very good at figuring out these changes.

A third pitfall of EVA is that our ranking systems are only as good as our estimates. If we estimate that for the next three years, Circus Circus will increase its EBITD at a 20 percent rate and its growth rate is 8 percent, we are not going to make much money. Getting that forecast as close as possible is critical.

Another pitfall is the difficulty of assessing reinvestment needs. These companies are constantly in the process of making deals. Comcast Corporation is nonstop, as are Tele-Communications Inc. (TCI) and Time Warner. Such deals are virtually impossible to predict, and they change the company's EVA matrix.

Despite all of its pitfalls, the EVA methodology offers many benefits. First, it is simple. All you need is
- to know where trailing EBITD is,
- to be able to subtract cash and add debt,
- to estimate hidden assets,
- to estimate how fast the company is going to grow.

Then, the last step is to rank the companies—a great way to make a living.

A second benefit is that the EVA method is logical. It is how bankers look at these industries.

Third, it is historically useful. We have been working with this approach for about five years, and it has helped us a great deal.

We have made very good investments but also some mistakes using EVA. We clearly stayed too long with the cable companies, believing the regulations would get better. Caesar's World, at five times EBITD and a 20 percent cash flow return, was tremendously cash generative, and ITT Corporation took the company out. Blockbuster Entertainment consistently had a value ratio exceeding 3 because it was growing at a very rapid rate.

We always thought Cap Cities was very expensive for good reason, but early this year, we noticed that the cash flow growth was changing dramatically. I called the company and said, "It looks as if you are generating $300 million a quarter of free cash." He said, "Yeah. Nobody else has noticed that." So we escalated the FCF growth rate on Cap Cities from 1 percent to 4 percent and it pushed the stock up enough on the matrix so that everybody decided it was a buy. About a month later, the company was taken over. An opportunity like that one is very good fortune, but being lucky always beats being smart.

Similarly, we became worried about Paramount in October. We were watching its films fail one after another. We lowered the three-year growth rate on Viacom from 17 or 20 to 14 because we also worried about Blockbuster. That made Viacom look very expensive. Recently, as the consolidated businesses of News Corp. have slowed dramatically, we have lowered that cash flow growth rate to practically nothing.

Conclusion

The media industry is very complex, and some mechanism is needed to simplify it. EVA is one such mechanism, but it is neither right nor wrong. If the market starts valuing Disney on an EPS (earnings per share) basis, the stock will probably be weak, and analysts like me could be wrong. I believe the EVA methodology is grounded in logic. It is where the future of our business is going, because these restructuring changes are being made by more than one company every day. EPS is less and less in tune with economic reality, and ultimately, economic reality is what determines common stock prices.

Question and Answer Session

Lawrence J. Haverty, Jr., CFA

Question: In your model, how do you value the fact that regulators are reviewing BSkyB's monopolistic practices? How do you view change in trends or fears?

Haverty: We try to come up with a discount factor, which is done very much by the seat of the pants. Currently, we are not involved in BSkyB, but we have watched it because we have been very close to News Corp. We are in contact with the British brokers, and we jiggle the rates periodically. The growth rate may be 40 now, but six months later it might be 20. We are worried about that possibility, but we try to capture it in the growth rates. We have pushed up our growth rates on cable because we think the industry is effectively undergoing deregulation.

Question: News Corp. is a sell in your ranking analysis, yet it has had one of the best strategic visions in the industry. How do you reconcile that anomaly?

Haverty: We are not involved in News Corp., but we watch it very carefully. I recently called the company to set up a meeting. You have to hold the company accountable for its plan. Star TV is a great vision, but it is not collecting any revenue. Ultimately, you have to look at cash. MCI Communications paid News Corp. $2 billion, which goes into the equity base. MCI now has News Corp. shares, so the shares have to go out and earn a return. News Corp. spent $700 million on a satellite auction, which gives them the right to spend another $1 billion to generate some cash flow three years after the satellite is launched. We are reasonably long-term investors, but Rupert Murdoch's time horizon is much longer than ours. I would rather be on the sidelines because I prefer to be paid sooner rather than later. Murdoch can partition the world and put News Corp. satellites up. Murdoch will have a satellite in almost every part of the world where there is income. We know how much BSkyB changed. BSkyB was once losing £6 million a week cash. Owning it is just a question of timing.

Question: Please explain why the Home Shopping Network (HSN) is at the bottom in your ratios, yet it has one of the highest growth rates.

Haverty: The company was not making any EBITD, and subsequently, it messed up my model because it had a negative EBITD, which is hard to do in this kind of a business. We put in an artificial EBITD, and HSN has a very high growth rate. Subsequently, a management implosion occurred and Barry Diller was brought in. HSN is currently very interesting, but in July, this stock was not interesting to us, and our model worked well at that time.

Question: How do you judge an acquisition at the time of announcement?

Haverty: This industry is management intensive, and we like to be very comfortable with management. Infinity Broadcasting recently announced an acquisition. I think the number is $275 million, and I think this entity has a trailing EBITD of 10. At 10, Infinity appears to have paid a little too much, but we know these guys too well. We sat down, and they gave us the cash flow numbers of what they expect that cash flow to be—say, up four times in three years. We know that their track record for acquisition analysis is good. The cash for the acquisition, $275 million, gets added to debt, and $10 million gets added to EBITD. That $10 million we figure will grow at a rate of, say, 60 percent over three years. The other $100 million of EBITD, we figure will grow at 20. Those two numbers are blended then to get a new ratio. Depending on whether that ratio is good or bad, we decide whether the acquisition is a good deal. We did this with Infinity, and it raised the value multiple by about 20 points, so we bought some stock. Now, a few months later, that move appears to have been a good idea. We are pretty comfortable as long as the company is doing something that it has been doing. We do not mind if Time Warner buys cable companies, but we probably would mind if they diverge from businesses in their range of competence.

Question: Don't your EVA and growth/value multiples ignore inherent differences in industry and company risks?

Haverty: This point is where the sociology comes in. The least risky industry in the whole pack is the gaming industry, yet it sells at the best value ratio. Wall Street is evaluating the industry wrong. Some industries, such as the apparel industry, are perceived to be of low quality. We have stock in The Warnaco Group and we have made a lot of money with them, because on a cash basis, it looked very attractive. You get a feeling of where an industry is likely to sell, you make a subjective judgment as to whether the market is assessing the risk of that industry efficiently, and then you put your money where your mouth is.

Question: What do you say to the Graham and Dodd investor who looks to book value or dividend streams? How do I ever get paid as a shareholder?

Haverty: I think you are in the wrong century. A guy once told me that book value was important for retailing. In retailing, most of book is inventory and receivables. In a liquidation, inventories are worth about 15 cents on the dollar—totally divorced from economic reality. Warren Buffett, a great espouser of Graham and Dodd, has used this form of analysis with his recent investments. He did very well with Cap Cities, he has done well with Coca-Cola, and he will be a big shareholder of the Disney Company. He has changed into a person who prefers cash flow protected with franchise. I do not particularly care with dividends whether the company gives it to me or not, but I do care when I see cash go away. I want the cash to be generated. We look at it every quarter, and we get very edgy when we start seeing companies run through cash. Book value is meaningless.

Question: Are rising private market value multiples good for stocks, given that they imply higher underlying asset values but may also imply lower returns on acquisition?

Haverty: I do not like private market values. Private market values go up and down with interest rates, and they are not a very good way to make a living. I invest in public markets, so I have to look at what that market is doing.

Question: Do you use any special accounting conventions for multi-industry and foreign companies such as News Corp., The Seagram Company, or Sony Corporation?

Haverty: Analysts who think they know everything should study Sony. They will find that they know nothing. You cannot follow Sony. It is not interested in people prying into its business. Its disclosure policies are inadequate. The ability to contact managers who know what they are doing is inadequate.

We found the exact opposite with News Corp. Because we thought the values were tremendous, we tried to obliterate the differences between Australian accounting and U.S. accounting. In Australia, at the end of the day, you win if you can find cash. In the United States, you win if you can find cash or value. In the case of BSkyB going up in value, the Australian accounting did not bother us. It bothered us a lot when we were getting into it. We felt we took a big risk but one that we were paid for handsomely. The company is very eager to have U.S. investors, and it is currently more a U.S. company than an Australian one. The risk for News Corp. is that it has a very low book and actual tax rate, and if the tax collectors could attach that income stream, the company might have some problems. If it were a U.S.-domiciled company, it would pay a much higher effective book and actual tax rate. That possibility is a risk in News Corp. that is not present in most other companies.

Question: Give us an example of a company that failed using your method and why.

Haverty: We were involved with Home Shopping Network, and we thought that it would earn $150 million in EBITD, but instead it earned $40 million. Our three-year EBITD growth rate was inopportune, and we lost some money. We stuck too long with the cable companies.

The Art of the Interview

John S. Reidy, CFA
Managing Director, Senior Analyst
Smith Barney, Inc.

Susan V. Watson, CFA
Vice President, Investor Relations
Gannett Company, Inc.

Successful analyst/company interviews are based on careful preparation, not on personal or investment firm attributes. Avoid excessively detailed, but irrelevant, questions. Do not try to contact upper level management without the assistance of the investor relations officer. In any event, the managers will probably know fewer details about the business than the IR officer. Because the economy, technology, and business conditions change, contacting the IR staff frequently is recommended.

Analyst: "Hi, this is Charlie Brown from Harriman & Ripley. I'll be in town tomorrow, and I want to see your CEO."

IR Manager: "He's not available tomorrow. Perhaps I can help you."

Analyst: "Listen, I am a large shareholder, and I'm not sure you have all the information I need."

IR Manager: "Well, sir, we have division of labor in this company. Mr. Curley manages the company, and I talk to the shareholders. I have some time available in the afternoon. Would you like to come in?"

Analyst: "Well, I'll need some time to get prepared. How about next Tuesday at 3 p.m.?"

IR Manager: "That will be fine. I look forward to seeing you then. Can I send you anything in advance? Do you have all the materials you need to review my company?"

Analyst: "I probably need the past two years' annual reports, 10-Ks, and quarterly statements."

IR Manager: "I'll also send you some monthly statistics; we release sales statistics every month. They might help you understand the current trends."

This dialogue between an analyst and an IR manager begins with a phone call from an inquisitive sell-side analyst. That someone would call and be this arrogant is hard to believe, but the trend is for some people to call and ask to speak directly to the CEO.

This presentation discusses the art of the interview—the right and wrong approaches to interviewing company investor relations (IR) staff members. The analysis applies equally to sell-side and to buy-side analysts.

Basic Rules

The scenario described above, although hypothetical and somewhat exaggerated, is not uncommon. The analyst in this dialogue has violated many of the cardinal rules in the art of an interview.

- *First rule*: Do not try to call on the CEO or the chief financial officer directly—go through the company's representative. If you do not, you will waste a lot of time and create antagonism.
- *Second rule*: Be prepared. Considering the material he asked for, Charlie Brown was not even prepared for an interview.
- *Third rule*: Don't expect special treatment. Even though Brown is with Harriman & Ripley, which manages billions of dollars, he has no more leverage than anybody else. The analyst

with a small account has the same entitlement to information as the analyst with a large account.

The staff in investor relations has the responsibility to make sure that disclosure is fair to everybody. Big accounts should not expect to be told more because they own more stock. If the CEO is not available to you, the chances are he is not available to anybody else on a regular basis. If the CEO is not regularly available, the company generally makes sure that its IR staff or operating managers have access to all the important information.

Preparation

Charlie Brown now has to prepare for an interview in a week. How does he do it? He looks at industry data from the government, the industry, and other sources. He reads the trade publications. The media industry has a proliferation of trade publications, and hot news will often be in the latest issues of *Advertising Age*, *Multichannel News*, or *Electronic Media*. The analyst also reads through the company's annual reports for the past couple of years, the latest 10-K, the current year's quarterly statements and 10-Qs, and any registration statements. Depending on the industry, the analyst might also call suppliers and competitors.

Many investor relations people wait for the analyst to ask the obvious questions suggested by these reports. By not asking those questions, the analyst gives the impression of not being prepared.

Questions for the Interview

Charlie Brown is now prepared and on the road for the face-to-face interview.

If the analyst's institution or firm has covered the stock before, it is a good idea (if possible) for the new analyst to go with his or her predecessor for the first visit. To avoid an approach completely at variance with the firm's previous strategy, the analyst who is taking over a stock should understand completely what his or her predecessor did.

Investor relations staff achieve no benefit by not being helpful. The IR person and the analyst are going to be in this relationship for a long time. If IR people help analysts along when they are new at the business, those analysts will remember. Such assistance will not change analysts' evaluations of the company, but they will form a lasting relationship with the IR person for that company.

The analyst's goal is not necessarily to become friends with the company's representative but to establish a long-standing working relationship. It may not be completely amicable, but it should not be adversarial.

One of the most important things for Charlie Brown to do is to arrive promptly and make friends with his company contact and that person's assistant or secretary. He wants to make that person his friend because when times are busy and the IR's assistant is assigning priorities to return phone calls, if he was a polite person last time, his name may stay near the top of the list. If he was rude, his call may not even get answered.

Now Charlie Brown arrives and begins the interview.

Analyst: "Hi, I'm Charlie Brown. I went to Princeton and Stanford Business School. I ran my own business for a few years. I'm a scratch golfer, and I was Phi Beta Kappa."

This is not a good way to start the interview. First, the IR manager does not care that he is a scratch golfer, that he went to Stanford, and so on. The information the IR manager will provide will not get any better because of Brown's credentials. More important is that Brown listen. I cannot tell you how many interviews I have had in which I did very little talking. You never learn anything while you are talking.

Also important is asking the appropriate questions. Charlie Brown may have spent a lot of time preparing for the interview, but the IR staff talk about the company all the time and have developed a certain understanding of what is important to analysts—in what fashion, in what order, and in what magnitude. Most IR managers will try to go through the business and explain what is important. Analysts can waste a lot of time on topics that will never affect their investment decisions. Often, the most productive approach is: "Tell me about your business." The analyst will get the important information in order of importance—where sales are coming from, how they are growing, why they are growing, which costs are important, what aspects of the business are obvious (and some that are not).

The disclosure levels among the media companies may vary dramatically, depending largely on how competitive the specific industry is. No company likes to give away the competitive goods. Some companies, such as the Gannett Company, are very willing to give the analyst chapter and verse on every newspaper every month because the towns where they do business have no other newspapers. The Walt Disney Company, on the other hand, will not help analysts with park attendance or ratings data. The competitive characteristics of Disney's business prevent it from revealing such information.

A great opener is: "Tell me about the corporate overview (or the corporate strategy)." This opener does not obtain answers to many questions ahead of time.

After the opening question and the IR person's overview, which has preempted some of the questions the analyst needs to ask, the analyst should turn to specific questions. Remember that minutiae will not determine the success of your investment advice. Some analysts go into excessive, meaningless detail. Analyzing those last five years' worth of quarterly radio ratings, for example, may be counterproductive.

Keep in mind why you are asking for each piece of information: Is it important? The most important questions relate to revenue and competition: What makes revenues grow—industry units, price, market share, new products, new services? Who is the competition?

The analyst should go through costs—variable costs, fixed costs, corporate overhead, expenses, financial interest, tax rates. What should be discussed will vary over time. Three years ago, the analyst probably would not have spent two minutes talking about the cost of newsprint, but in visiting Gannett today, that topic would be important.

The discussion of finances continues with cash versus book value, shares, range of earnings, and so forth. One issue for conducting the interview is getting down to what the earnings number will be. Rather than saying something like, "I think earnings will be $3.25," an old technique analysts use is to say, "By the way, we are just getting under way on this. What is the consensus on earnings?" Phrasing the question this way allows the IR person to give guidance on the company's prevailing earnings expectations without giving the company's official forecast. The consensus earnings expectation is not likely to vary dramatically from what the company thinks at a given time.

The analyst is collecting a lot of numbers and should keep in mind that the result is often a 27-page earnings model that is no more accurate than a 1-page summary recommendation on whether to buy or sell the stock. Sell-side analysts may have to produce the model to prove that they know what they are doing, but many investors do not need a lengthy earnings model. On the contrary, such detail may even get in the way of the overall picture.

Some numbers an analyst cannot avoid are those on the balance sheet and the funds flow statement. We spend a lot less time than we should in interviews talking about the balance sheet and perhaps too much time talking about the income statement.

Follow the money or, more importantly, follow the cash. Where are the dollars coming from in that figure on earnings before interest, taxes, depreciation, and amortization (EBITDA)? What is the company doing with the money? Where is it going? Is it for acquisitions? Is there any cash in the first place? A company can have lots of earnings and no free cash. As the discussion moves into where the cash is going, other issues pertaining to corporate strategies, such as acquisitions and divestiture, are likely to come up.

The analyst will have examined long-term and short-term debt and perhaps have been able to pencil in a funds flow statement. Of course, if the company has hidden assets, the analyst must estimate their potential value. The example of Turner Broadcasting System stock is apt. At the moment, it does not contribute meaningfully to either Liberty Media or Time Warner's cash flow, but it clearly has potential value.

The analyst would want to make some adjustment for that situation and would ask the IR person for guidance on which businesses among the hidden assets are losing money. Right now, for example, in the case of Gannett and Knight-Ridder, Brown would put the Detroit newspaper situation on a separate page for separate analysis. The analyst can adjust the cash flow analysis accordingly. Suppose, for example, *Entertainment Weekly* is losing $25 million. Rather than saying it will be worth $0.5 billion in ten years, Brown could take its loss out of his cash flow analysis on the theory that it is a developmental business.

Another point the analyst should note is how a company talks about its earnings, about the financial results of its endeavors. When a company goes from reporting earnings per share (EPS) to EBITDA by division, something has happened. Why is the company talking about EBITDA? Do you care about EBITDA because you want to put everybody on the same basis, or do you want to consider that some companies' EBITDA is not all going to be turned back into capital, or interest expense, or something else?

A very important point is that Charlie Brown should have some idea about how the financial community values the company. Whether he agrees with that measure is a different issue. The analyst must examine all the measures of value and determine which one will be most compelling.

Therefore, Brown has to have them all, but going from EBITDA to earnings to after-tax or free cash flow is not hard. If Charlie Brown goes into Tele-Communications Inc. to talk about EPS, he will be ushered out the door because that discussion will not take place. Most analysts try to have everything on an EBITDA basis in at least one place, but comparing Gannett's EBITDA with the EBITDA of a growing cable company or of a broadcasting company may not be very meaningful.

A number that is not of great value is a per share cash flow number that does not take into account either interest expense or debt. What good is knowing that a company had $100 million in cash flow and 10 million shares (so cash flow per share is $10) if it has $1 billion of debt? Beware of reports and analyses that focus only on cash flow per share without annotating either the attributable debt or the attributable interest (or, in some cases, taxes) expensed to it.

As one wraps up the discussion of the balance sheet, an obvious question is: "What kind of financing needs do you have?" The analyst does not want to recommend the XYZ Company and have the company a month later unexpectedly have an offering that increases the number of shares by 25 percent. Analysts may have to work hard on getting this information because some IR staff are quite reticent about telling analysts all the company's financing needs.

Conclusion

From the IR perspective, what an analyst should do and not do in the major interview can be boiled down to ten pieces of advice:

- Unless you count the CEO among your in-laws—and maybe even if you do—assume that the IR officer is your best ally in the company.
- The size of your portfolio does not determine the quality and quantity of information you will get.
- Do not try to contact managers behind the IR officer's back. If they want to talk to you—and many times they do not—the IR officer can arrange it. In general, if the company cannot do it for everybody else, it will not do it for Charlie Brown.
- Sometimes the analyst's earnings model is more accurate than the company's estimate for the simple reason that it is more objective. The company wraps up its vision, hopes, wishes, dreams, and goals in its estimate, which could thus be biased. In addition, companies do not revise their budgets every three weeks in response to ordinary events. So, keep in mind that the analyst may be ahead of the curve on the company in relation to certain assumptions. The practical reason for the companies to have budgets is to motivate the managers to run the business as efficiently as possible. Top managers are not going to reduce the pressure at the beginning of the year simply because one cost looks as if it might go down. Sometimes analysts' needs and company needs differ, and companies may not have revised estimates ready because of a crisis in some part of the company.
- Be polite and be prepared. Most IR staff will reciprocate.
- When you have meetings with the CEOs, try to make the meetings interesting for them, too. IR staff specialize in minutia. The company chairs, CEOs, or presidents do not carry such data around in their heads. They have other things to take up their time. Moreover, the IR person can ask for only a limited amount of the CEO's time. Analysts are unlikely to be visiting a CEO until after the IR staff has had a chance to meet them and has obtained a general impression of who they are, what they do, and how much they know. The IR people do not want the CEO to be surprised or embarrassed. They want to ensure that the analysts can hold up their end of the conversation. Most CEOs are open to talking to someone who can say something more interesting than "What is your interest expense going to be next quarter?" The analyst's spreadsheet is not a good place to start—or finish.
- Sarcasm is never welcome in a group meeting. Not long ago, a relatively new analyst to the industry raised his hand in a meeting with 200 people and said to the chair, "Last month you met with us and said your earnings were going to be x. Now, you are telling us earnings are going to be $x - 1$." The unspoken question was, "Don't you know enough about your business to give us the right answer both times?" What it sounded like to the rest of the people attending the meeting was: "Were you lying to us then, or are you lying to us now?"
- Remember that managing a company is different from managing a portfolio. Unlike portfolios, companies cannot be bought in the morning and sold in the afternoon.
- Don't assume that the IR manager knows the future and just won't tell you what it holds. The IRs are as uncertain about the future as the analysts.

- Things change. Stay in touch with the IR staff.

The worst thing an analyst can do is say something impolite about management in the press. Even it is true, mention of it should be avoided in the press. The company may never forgive and never forget. An analyst once wrote a report about a company, and although she thought it was very reasonable and was not trying to be particularly negative, she made a comment on what she thought the company's long-term earnings growth would be. It has been five years, and the company's chair has never let her forget it. The fact that she was wrong did not make it any better.

Question and Answer Session

John S. Reidy, CFA
Susan V. Watson, CFA

Question: How willing are IR staff to share information on or impressions of the competition, such as other newspaper companies?

Watson: I am frequently quite willing to share such information, and I suspect other companies are also. We hear gossip, and we pass it along; of course, it may not be true and should be labeled as such, but it is interesting. People often ask me what I think about some information because I used to be an analyst in this industry. I will not analyze another company for you, but I will explain why factors that are important to you may be less important to somebody else. That willingness depends on the IR person, however.

Question: A company once offered me its own earnings model; is such an offer common?

Reidy: I do not recall that ever happening. It might occur when you are doing due diligence on a company that is considering going public.

Watson: I would be suspicious. As I said, don't assume we know the future and simply will not tell you. Your estimate may be more valid than my budget. Just because I think something will happen does not mean it will. I would also be concerned with the legalities. Those 10b-5 violations can be very expensive.

Reidy: I would view the company with considerable skepticism. We can usually develop better books then they can.

Watson: When I was an analyst and Taft Broadcasting was still public, I wrote an analysis in which I kept referring to its earnings performance as "better than planned." This phrase got the Taft IR person in trouble because it implied that I had seen the plan; I was using it simply to indicate that the actual performance was different from my estimate. So, analysts need to be sensitive to the language they use.

Question: When should an analyst ask to meet with operating management?

Watson: You can ask any time you want, but the answer will vary. We do not make operating management available to anybody. Several times a year, we bring the head of the Newspaper Division or the head of the Broadcasting Division to make a group presentation, but no one has visited them in their offices in my ten years with the company. The managers do not have the time; if 150 analysts follow Gannett and they all want to see the head of our Newspaper Division, he will not have time to run the division.

Reidy: I would probably ask to see the chief financial officer or a strategic planner. The answer to that request would be made on the basis of his or her time and my perceived degree of interest.

Field trips are the best opportunities to meet managers in a company. Also, several people from each of the media companies attend the PaineWebber seminars, the newspaper publishers sponsor a midyear conference, and almost all the media companies have speakers that they make available. Buttonholing them after an industry presentation is acceptable.

Question: Where do you draw the line for guidance?

Watson: I see the forecasts published every month in *First Call*. If a number for Gannett is way out of line—high or low—I will occasionally call and say, "You are way out of the consensus range. Can we talk about how you got there?" We have always had a "no surprises" policy at Gannett. We will do whatever it takes to help analysts tune their earnings models, and then we will work like dogs operationally to get to those numbers.

An analyst who talks to me regularly will not be out of tune because the odds are, just to make sure, I will end the conversation with, "So, what is your estimate these days?" But analysts have to take some responsibility and call me; I cannot read their minds. We send out a monthly revenue sheet to 500 people, and it should jog their memories: If your estimate is up 20 percent for the quarter and you see revenues go down three months in a row, you should wonder what is wrong.

Question: A common perception is that sell-side or large institutions get preferential treatment—in getting called back prior to conference calls, getting better access to information, or getting better seating at company lunches or dinners. How do you respond to that perception?

Watson: Giving preference is

not intentional, but sometimes it happens because we know the sell-side people: They call us more, and they come around more frequently. Like anyone else, managers want to sit with somebody they know and are comfortable with. The information given, however, will not be different. We are scrupulous about the materiality issue at Gannett. In fact, all telephone calls are time-stamped and returned in order—there are no preferences.

Reidy: A small institution may not initially receive the attention given a major buy-side analyst, but if the analyst continues to take an interest in the company, he or she will get the same information. If the stock is important to the analyst, the analyst will get important treatment from the company.

Question: I work for a small West Coast money manager; can the interview be handled by telephone, or is an on-site visit necessary?

Watson: I often have telephone interviews that last an hour or more, and if that is not enough time, we can do another interview the next day. It is a good idea to call in advance and make an appointment for a telephone interview. If you want to hook up two or three money managers on the other end, which is much more efficient than flying people in from different locations, I will also do that.

Reidy: One useful approach for visits after the first interview is to prepare an updated model and send it to the IR staff in advance of either a subsequent telephone interview or visit and give them a week to look at it. You can save time later. But don't send a 27-page model.

Watson: I once received—from an analyst in training—15 iterations of an earnings model that was 20 pages long. It was hard to see the difference from one iteration to another, and because we had not had any substantive conversation about the business, I could not discern the thought process behind the model changes. It was an enormous waste of time.

Question: When asking open-ended questions, how can we be sure the company is not telling us only the positive side of the story?

Watson: You must think, listen, and evaluate the information. I will give you all the facts, good and bad, but you must analyze this information. You must make the decision. If you think you are getting only the good side, challenge me. Ask me what could go wrong. I have ten things that could go wrong on any given day. If you want, I will help you assign a probability to those things, but you have to ask me. I will tell you the bad possibilities as well as the good possibilities because if the bad happens and you are surprised, you will never trust me again.

Reidy: On both the buy side and the sell side, analysts have two jobs. One is to assemble some sort of model of the numbers; the second is to then decide whether the stock is a buy, sell, or hold. The IR staff cannot help with that second task, partly because the decision depends on comparing one set of numbers with alternative investments.

Watson: Sometimes, you will like the stock, and other times, you will not. Treating you differently when you don't like the stock has no value for the IR officer because the time will come when your decision will go the other way. The different treatment will have poisoned the relationship.